THE ISSACHAR FACTOR

*Understanding
Trends That Confront
Your Church
And Designing A
Strategy For Success*

GLEN MARTIN &
GARY MCINTOSH

BROADMAN
& HOLMAN
PUBLISHERS

Nashville, Tennessee

0-8054-2017-7
Dewey Decimal Classification: 254.6
Subject Heading: CHURCH RENEWAL // MINISTRY, CHRISTIAN
Library of Congress Card Catalog Number: 93-31202
Printed in the United States of America

Unless otherwise stated, all Scripture quotations are from the Holy Bible, *New International Version,* copyright 1973, 1978, 1984 by International Bible Society. Scripture quotations marked (NASB) are from the *New American Standard Bible,* © The Lockman Foundation, 1960, 1962, 1963, 1968, 1971, 1972, 1973, 1975, 1977, used by permission; and (NKJV) from the *New King James Version,* copyright © 1979, 1980, 1982, Thomas Nelson, Inc., Publishers.

Library of Congress Cataloging-in-Publication Data

McIntosh, Gary, 1947–
    The issachar factor : understanding trends that confront your church and designing a strategy for success / Garly L. McIntosh and Glen S. Martin.
        p. cm.
    Includes bibliographical references.
    ISBN 0-8054-2017-7 (pb)
    ISBN 0-8054-3014-8 (hc)
    1. Church leadership.   2. Church growth.   3. Pastoral theology.
I. Martin, Glen, 1953–   .   II. Title.
BV652.1.M39   1994
253—dc20   93-31202
                                                                          CIP

1 2 3 4 5 02 01 00 99

*"The Sons of Issachar
understood the times and knew
what Israel should do."*

1 Chronicles 12:32

To our wives:
Nancy Martin
Carol McIntosh

and our children
Kerry, Scott, and David Martin
Gary and Aaron McIntosh

who are our inspiration and support
in doing His ministry as a team.

CONTENTS

1

To prophesy is extremely difficult
especially with respect to the future.
——Chinese Proverb

[The] Men of Issachar, . . . understood the times
and knew what Israel should do.
——1 Chronicles 12:32

MINISTRY

When Charles Haddon Spurgeon first went to Park Street Church in London, he was nineteen years old. There he found a church with a seating capacity of fifteen hundred but with an attendance of under two hundred. Nine years later the Metropolitan Tabernacle was built to accommodate the crowds which came to hear him preach; his sermons were published in newspapers around the world; a school had been established to train pastors; and a Colportage business was started to print evangelistic booklets. It is said that over 23,000 people had heard him preach during those years.

During Spurgeon's thirty-eight years as pastor of the Metropolitan Tabernacle, his congregation included six thousand worshipers and added fourteen thousand members. Clearly the Metropolitan Tabernacle was one of the most influential churches of the nineteenth century.

In 1972, however, seventy-five years after Charles Haddon Spurgeon retired, some pastors visiting his church counted only eighty-seven worshipers present for the morning service!

What had happened to this once great church? In simple terms, it hadn't changed with the times. London had changed; people had changed; but the church's approach to ministry had remained the same. Gradually, people left and fewer people came until the Metropolitan Tabernacle was no longer effective in reaching people for Christ.

We live and minister in changing times. The following comments, which pastors have made to us in seminars throughout the United States, illustrate the changing times in which we live:

▲ People are coming and going in my community so fast that I feel like I'm preaching to a parade.

▲ I'm faced with co-dependency, divorce recovery, blended families, and all kinds of physical and emotional abuse issues. Seminary didn't prepare me for this. I need help!

▲ When I finally feel like I make the ends meet, someone moves the ends.

▲ How can I meet people's needs when I don't even understand their needs?

▲ We say we've got the answer, but they're not even asking the question.

▲ I seem to be able to touch people's heads but not their hearts.

We do live in changing times, and, for better or worse, church ministry isn't what it used to be. Dramatic changes in our society are forcing us to re-examine how we do ministry. In bygone eras we conducted ministry in one basic way; today, it's literally a whole new ball game. What are some of the changes that have taken place in our society which have affected our churches? And, most importantly, what can we do to be more effective in finding, keeping, and building people for our Lord Jesus Christ?

Before we begin to address individual areas, it is necessary to indulge in a bit of groundwork. What happened in the last quarter century to even make changes in ministry necessary?

Changing Ages

Social scientists have identified three distinct ages which serve as a brief outline of history: the agricultural age, the industrial age, and the information age. Roughly each of these ages spans a period of time when families, work, and society shared essential qualities.

The agricultural age refers to the time period which spanned most of known history to about 1860. Named for the main occupation of over 90 percent of all workers—the main context was the small rural town. The key unit was the extended family.[1]

The industrial age covers the time period from 1860 to about 1956. With the rise of industrial factories, the main context was the city. The key unit was the nuclear family.

The information age began about 1956 and continues to the present. Named for the rapid increase of information, the main context is the world. The key unit is the fractured family. (See fig. 1.1)

Comparison of Ages

	Agricultural	Industrial	Information
Dates	? to 1860	1860 to 1956	1956 to present
Context	Town	City	World
Work	Farm	Factory	Office
Job	Farmer	Worker	Manager
Family	Extended	Nuclear	Fractured

Figure 1.1

During the last half century, we have lived in a virtual explosion of information. More information has been produced in the last thirty years than in the previous five thousand. Today, information doubles every five years. By the year 2000 it will be doubling every four years! For example, note the following signs of the information explosion experienced since the 1940s.[2]

▲ *Computers:* Between 1946 and 1960 the number of computers grew from one to ten thousand, and from 1960 to 1980 to ten million. By the year 2000 there will be over eighty million computers in the United States alone. The number of components that can be programmed into a computer chip is doubling every eighteen months.[3]

▲ *Publications:* Approximately ninety-six hundred different periodicals are published in the United States each year, and about one thousand books are published internationally

9

every day. Printed information doubles every eight years. A weekday edition of the New York Times contains more information than the average person was likely to come across in a lifetime in seventeenth century England.[4]

▲ *Libraries:* The world's great libraries are doubling in size every fourteen years. In the early 1300s, the Sorbonne Library in Paris contained only 1,338 books and yet was thought to be the largest library in Europe. Today several libraries in the world have an inventory of well over eight million books each.[5]

▲ *Periodicals:* The Magazine Publishers Association notes that 265 more magazines were published in 1988 than in 1989, which works out to about one a day if magazine creators take weekends off. Newsstands offer a choice of twenty-five hundred different magazines. [6]

▲ *Reference works:* The Pacific Bell Yellow pages are used about 3.5 million times a day. There are 33 million copies of 108 different directories with 41 billion pages of information. The new second edition of the *Random House Dictionary of the English Language* contains more than 315,000 words, has 2,500 pages, weighs 13.5 pounds, and has 50,000 new entries.[7]

All of this information is good. Right? Wrong! Today we must deal with new challenges like overload amnesia, which occurs when an individual's brain shuts down to protect itself. Did you ever forget simple information like a friend's name when trying to introduce them to another person? That's overload amnesia. Or have you ever crammed for an exam only to forget what it was about less than one hour later? That's "Chinese-dinner memory dysfunction"—an undue emphasis on short-term memory. Or have you ever read about an upcoming event in a church program only to forget about it later? That's a result of "informational cacophony"—too much exposure to information so that you end up reading or hearing something but not remembering it. Finally, consider VCRitis— buying a high-technology product, getting it home, and then not being able to program it.

Exposure to this proliferation of information has created a generation of people with different needs, needs which require new models of ministry. The problem is that many churches continue to use models of ministry which do not address the different needs people have today. Examine the following effects of the information age. Ministry must change to meet people's needs today.

▲ People have less free time, and are more difficult to recruit.

▲ People oppose change, resist making friends, and are lonely.

▲ People are bombarded by so much information that they find it difficult to listen to more information.

▲ People cannot see the big picture, tie the ends together, or see how the pieces relate.

▲ People hear more than they understand, forget what they already know, and resist learning more.

▲ People don't know how to use what they learn, make mistakes when they try, and fell guilty about it.

▲ People know information is out there, have difficulty getting it, and make mistakes without it.

Changing Models

Even though we minister in the information age, churches continue to reflect their agricultural and industrial age roots. This leads to stress as programs that worked in the past are not as effective today. Consider these two examples.

Worship services at 11:00 A.M. are a throwback to the agricultural age when churches had to give farmers time to complete the morning chores, hitch the horse to the wagon, and drive into town. The time most farmers completed this routine, 11:00 A.M., was the logical choice for morning church services to begin. Today, however, many churches find earlier hours for worship services often attract more people.

The evening service is a throwback to the industrial age when electric lights were first developed. Initially not every home or business establishment was able to have lights installed. Some enterprising church leaders found that by installing electric lights they could attract crowds to evening evangelistic church services. Today many churches find that smaller groups meeting in homes attract more people than evening services.

Let's face it: Most church models of ministry were developed in an entirely different age. The models of ministry developed in the agricultural and industrial ages are colliding head-on with the information age. That's what this book is all about. Our nation has changed; people have changed; and we must develop new models of ministry relevant for today's society if we are to fulfill Christ's commission to "make disciples."

While it is not possible to cover every aspect of ministry, throughout this book you'll find not only insight as to what changes have taken place, but also practical ideas you can use immediately to be more effective in your own ministry .

To get the best value from this book first overview the entire contents. You will find that each chapter focuses on areas of ministry commonly found in churches. If you are involved in a ministry specifically addressed by one chapter, read that chapter first and begin to use some of the practical suggestions immediately. Then go back through the other chapters, carefully noting insights and ideas applicable to other ministries in your church.

People of Issachar

In the Old Testament there's an interesting story in 1 Chronicles 12. David had been running from Saul, and while he was hiding, God sent some men to him who are described as mighty men of valor. The first group of men were skilled with the bow, with the arrow, and with the sling. These men would stand behind the lines and shoot arrows and fling stones over the front lines to inflict wounds on the enemy. Other men were skilled in the use of the shield and the sword, moved swiftly, and had a tenacious spirit. They would fight one on one with the enemy at the front lines. A third category of men understood the times and knew what Israel should do. They were the strategists who developed the master plan for the battle. We today need to be like men of Issachar. We need to be people who understand our times, know what we should do, and have the courage to do it.

We trust that *The Issachar Factor* will help you understand the times in which you are called to minister and know what to do to increase your church's effectiveness.

▼

Decades Make a Difference

What's hot and what's not? It often seems to change with the decades. Complete the last line of each of the following groups to see how things have changed since the sixties.

1. 60s: Cassius Clay
   70s: Muhammed Ali
   80s: Mike Tyson
   90s: _____

2. 60s: Hare Krishnas
   70s: Street mimes
   80s: Break dancers
   90s: _____

3. 60s: Troll dolls
   70s: Pet rocks
   80s: Garfield in the window
   90s: _____

4. 60s: Life
   70s: Time
   80s: Wall Street Journal
   90s: _____

5. 60s: Frostee Freeze
   70s: 31 flavors
   80s: Haagen Das
   90s: _____

6. 60s: Converse
   70s: Adidas
   80s: Reebok
   90s: _____

7. 60s: Hippies
   70s: Preppies
   80s: Yuppies
   90s: _____

8. 60s: VW Bug with harmonica
   70s: Anything with cassette stereo
   80s: BMW with CD player
   90s: _____

9. 60s: Governor Ronald Reagan
   70s: Candidate Ronald Reagan
   80s: President Ronald Reagan
   90s: _____

10. 60s: Fondue
    70s: Quiche
    80s: Sushi
    90s: _____

11. 60s: KJV
    70s: NASB
    80s: NIV
    90s: _____

12. 60s: Gurus
    70s: Astrologers
    80s: Channelers
    90s: _____

13. 60s: Drive-in movies
    70s: Drive-in fast food
    80s: Drive-in ATM
    90s: _____

14. 60s: Civil rights
    70s: Women's rights
    80s: Animal rights
    90s: _____

15. 60s: Wonder Bread
    70s: Ten-Grain Bread
    80s: Oat Bran Bread
    90s: _____

16. 60s: TV
    70s: Video games
    80s: Home computers
    90s: _____

17. 60s: Mini-skirts
    70s: Mini-series
    80s: Mini-vans
    90s: _____

18. 60s: Picket lines
    70s: Gas lines
    80s: Church lines
    90s: _____

NOTES

[1] Two hundred years ago 95 percent of the U.S. work force was involved in farming. Today less than 4 percent of our work force is farming. By 1900, 25 percent of the U.S. work force was in factories. By 1950, 65 percent of the workforce was in factories. Today only 15 percent of the workforce is in factories.–"Customer Satisfaction," *Learning Network Magazine* (Minneapolis: Performax Learning Network, October, 1988), 2.

[2] Richard Saul Wurman, *Information Anxiety* (New York: Doubleday, 1989), 32.

[3] George Shultz, quoted by Wurman, 41 and 309.

[4] Ibid., 34– 35. Also see Alvin Toffler, *Future Shock* , 30-31.

[5] Wilbur Shramm and William Porter, quoted by Wurman, 206.

[6] William B. Geist, "Magazine Chaos: From Hot Tubs to Talking Birds," *The New Times*, May 20,1987.

[7] Wurman, 79, 118.

2

A wise investor turns spare time into prayer time.
—Sign on a church wall

Lord, teach us to pray just as John taught his disciples.
—Luke 11:1

PRAYER

Tim was an active member of our collegian group and appeared to be on his way into the ministry. His heart was right, yet there was one aspect of his life that deeply troubled him—his mother. He could remember growing up in the church and his mom taking him to every service and every event. But now his mother had withdrawn from the church and, even more *frightening*, from life. She spent all her time in her room with little contact with her two sons and husband.

Unknown to the family, this all started after her association with another woman who had advised her to renounce her husband's authority and submit to her own authority. This very unbiblical advice caused trouble in many areas of her life, and now the entire family was struggling.

A director of prayer and personal intercessor at a large church in southern California met with Tim and committed to pray for him and his family every day. The intercessor also traveled to their home to pray "on-site." She knew that prayer was the only tool that would break down these walls of silence and exclusion.

One week from the initial contact, Tim's mom, who had previously only communicated with the family through notes, sat down with her son to talk for the first time in three years. She shared that she had just realized that she was in trouble and needed help, but that she did not know what she could do.

First, Tim shared Christ with his mother and she accepted Him as her Savior. Then a weekly time was set up for the intercessor to meet and pray for Tim's mother. Two weeks later Tim's father came for counseling because of the changes seen in his wife's life. The family then decided to hold a birthday party for Tim's mother as she had essentially missed the last three years. At the birthday party at their church, Tim's grandmother received the Lord.

What do these three people have in common? *Prayer.* Their lives had been changed because of the prayer life of an intercessor.

Prayer

That was then...	This is now...
▲ Mid-week prayer	▲ Early morning prayer
▲ Prayer warriors	▲ Prayer intercessors
▲ Cottage prayer	▲ Small group prayer
▲ Little prayer education	▲ Much prayer education
▲ Pastoral prayer time	▲ Individual prayer time
▲ A strength of churches	▲ A weakness of churches
▲ Every pastor prays	▲ Directors of prayer
▲ Prayer at the end of counseling	▲ Prayer as an ingredient to counseling
▲ Obligation to pray	▲ Burden to pray
▲ Prayer lists	▲ Conversational prayer
▲ Praying defensively	▲ Praying offensively
▲ Opening prayers for a service	▲ Prayer teams during service
▲ Prayer accountability	▲ Prayer journaling
▲ Prayer partners	▲ Prayer triads
▲ Low profile for prayer	▲ Higher prayer visibility

In the early 1700s, the Moravians pushed for worldwide change in Europe. Their motivation was Zinzendorf's desire to provide aid for the followers of Martin Luther. Within the "holy huddle" of Zinzendorf's protection, the theological diversity became too much to handle, so disputes and infighting became prominent. Soon they concluded that prayer was the only answer.

Thus began what historians call the Moravian Prayer Vigil. It did not take long for this localized movement to spread across the world. Men like Jonathan Edwards and John Wesley caught the vision, and the movement spread westward, resulting in the lay ministry Wesley titled "Societies." It was in these small groups that prayer became an active part of neighborhood meetings.

By the 1800s frontier revivalism continued in the format of concerts of prayer. These were designed to promote unity and a more aggressive evangelistic outreach throughout the frontier. In England, many denominations would gather on the first Monday of each month to pray for revival. As survival became more pressing in the Americas, unity of purpose as well as concern were mandatory. Prayer became the catalyst: in the 1800s, as the springboard for missionary societies; and the 1900s, the era of expansion.

Another vital ingredient that provided momentum for the 1900s was the "noon prayer hour." Expansion had already begun, and religious as well as secular society was excited about the newfound vision. In response to the people's gratitude and hope, people held prayer meetings, devoting an hour at lunch to read Scripture and pray. In Portland, Oregon, businessmen agreed to close for two hours each afternoon to provide adequate time for employees to gather and pray. Men such as Charles Spurgeon, Hudson Taylor, and Dwight L. Moody, and organizations such as the Salvation Army were a direct result of this revival of prayer.

The mid-1900s brought in a whole new approach to evangelism, with outreach now centered at a rally. Billy Graham crusades addressed abuse, violence, crime, and immorality.

In Korea, under the leadership of Dr. Paul Yonggi Cho and other men of God, untold thousands came to Christ with an emphasis placed on prayer. At prayer mountains, small cubicles or caves were constructed so people could be alone with God and intercede for themselves and their nation. Many believe that these prayer warriors are a key reason why tiny South Korea has been able to survive the North Korean takeover.

But that was then and this is now. Significant changes are also taking place today.

Prayer Trends

We live in one of the greatest prayer revivals of modern history. It is by far the most comprehensive, far-reaching, and fastest learning curves recently experienced in the spiritual discipline of prayer. We have observed the following twelve prayer trends which may give you ideas for increasing prayer in your own ministry.

1. Praying the Scripture

Although the concept seems foreign to most believers, praying the Scriptures provides a meaningful avenue for revealing needs and finding biblical solutions. God is in the process of reshaping our thinking, values, and lives to become more Christ-like. Through the Scriptures God puts His finger on a need; and we can use these Scriptures as a pattern to pray so that our lives will be shaped according to His will. Praying the Scriptures, therefore, is a way of helping us pray directly according to God's will. How is it that the Scripture can change the shape of our lives? A simple acrostic can help even the young believer pray more effectively as he uses God's Word in prayer. When reading your Bible, ask yourself, "Is there a…"

> Sin to confess?
> Habit to correct?
> Attitude to change?
> Promise to claim?
> Example to copy?

As we have already noted, time is the new commodity in the 1990s. People do not want to waste their time in praying for irrelevant things. They like to get right to the heart of the matter. Praying the Scriptures can help them pray directly according to God's will: "This is the assurance we have in approaching God: that if we ask anything according to his will, he hears us. And if we know that he hears us—whatever we ask—we know that we have what we ask of him" (1 John 5:14–15). When we pray Scripture, we know that He not only hears us because this is His revealed will, but He also answers us.

2. Concerts of Prayer

A concert of prayer is the uniting of the entire local body of Christ in prayer for the things that concern God. On a more practical level a concert of prayer unites pastors, leaders, and churches—cross-denominationally—in prayer for the spiritual awakening of their community, city, etc. Typically, these concerts are orchestrated to concentrate on two specific areas: revival and outreach. David Bryant, a longtime missions expert for InterVarsity and member of the National Prayer Committee, has been in the forefront of encouraging these concerts to be established in many cities. To devote more time to this effort, he left InterVarsity and formed his own concert of prayer organization.

One reason for success in this movement is that it breaks down the traditional separation and misconceptions between denominations, as seen most prominently between the charismatics and evangelicals. Those who would never think of cooperating closely with others of a different theological persuasion find that not only can they pray with such people, but these people from the "other side of the fence" also have a heart for God and a rich prayer life. So a growing appreciation and respect occurs in both camps. Such cooperation in prayer is often a forerunner for cooperation in other areas and a step toward the unity Jesus prays for in John 17.

A noteworthy example of an active, well-organized concert of prayer movement is in Los Angeles. Here many strong, well-recognized pastors across denominational lines have gathered to focus intensive prayer on the needs of the greater Los Angeles area. They meet once a month for two hours.

Pastors Jack Hayford and Lloyd Ogilvie co-lead these meetings. They usually present a ten- to fifteen-minute devotional challenge and encouragement, together with worship and singing. Over 50 percent of the time is spent in praying for the needs of their area, although not for specific religious groups, churches, or organizations. Instead, they pray for the needs of the churches in general but specifically—evangelism, finances, holy life of staff, and congregations, and unity.

They also focus much attention on the needs of the city—drugs, violence, homelessness. A representative from the city or a group working in the needy area may present five minutes of background and prayer requests so that the group will better know how to pray. Since this group consists of about eighteen hundred pastors and Christian leaders from a large southern California area, they encourage smaller groups to form in localized areas, often to organize a specific prayer outreach.

3. Praise

Another area of prayer that has come into its own today is praise. People are learning the power of this tool when used rightly.

We have traditionally used praise only at a level of worshiping God for who He is and what He does. But praise can go beyond that level to become a real weapon against the enemy and to intensify our prayer life. How can this be done?

First, praise helps us focus our heart on God. It helps us put into a right perspective who He is and what He has and can do. This is important, especially when we are going through times of difficulty. As we see praise change our perspective we also can see something else happening: praise becomes a way of intercepting the darts of the enemy and causing him to cease his attacks. David knew this principle. In the Psalms he not only focused on who God is, but frequently as he praised Him, David's attitude about his circumstances changed.

Second, praise removes worry and earthly concerns. Many times our focus is on earthly responsibilities and extraneous activities, as well as our circumstances. We close our eyes and try to pray, but we are overwhelmed by a long list of wants and needs. Our world seems to be closing in on us.

People are flocking to the psychiatrist for help. Depression and suicide are rampant at all ages. In April of 1991, a local news special report concerned the deterioration of public education, as seen in the sad results of surveys among high school students. According to this televised report, 6 percent of all high school students in 1990 admitted to having tried or at least thought seriously of suicide.

Praise can help overcome this level of despondency. People can take their eyes off their problems and focus on the God who is all powerful, good, and loving. As Wesley Duewel, in *Mighty Prevailing Prayer*, said: "[Praise] shuts you in with God and His angels."

Third, praise increases faith. To praise God is to become more aware of God. To become more aware of God is to recognize not only His greatness, but also His faithfulness.

A person comes to realize, "the same God who parted the seas for Moses, will part the troubled waters that I am in. The same God who provided a promised land for Israel, has a promised plan for me." He can agree with the apostle Paul, "Being confident of this, that he who began a good work in you will carry it on to completion until the day of Christ Jesus" (Phil. 1:6). As confidence grows, a person feels secure to trust Him for even greater things.

Fourth, praise invades Satan's territory. Praise is one of the least recognized of the prayer weapons we have to defeat the enemy, yet it is powerful and able to make Satan flee when used in the right way. Some Christian leaders are convinced that Satan once was the leader of the praise and worship in heaven. Thus when we praise God we are reminding Satan from where he has fallen. He hates praise so much that he flees when he hears intense praising of God. Those who practice this type of spiritual battling often report greater victories in prayer and a lessening of the attacks on them.

These four results of praise are illustrated in Paul's words to the Philippians: "Do not be anxious about anything, but in everything, by prayer and petition, *with thanksgiving,* present your requests to God" (Phil. 4:6, emphasis added).

One of Satan's foremost attacks against the believer is the creation of worry. In these situations praise becomes the articulation of faith. Do you remember the story of Paul and Silas? For doing what was right before God, they were thrown in jail. Of course, the local magistrates felt that Paul was disrupting the economy, so they were beaten, chained, and confined. How did they handle that situation? The Book of Acts says that they prayed. But that's not all. The verse continues that they were, "singing hymns to God, and the other prisoners were listening to them" (Acts 16:25).

What did Paul and Silas do in a life-and-death situation where the enemy had the upper hand? They sang praises to God loud enough for the entire facility to hear. And the result was that a violent earthquake shook the prison, chains were loosed, and the doors were opened. It was as though God was anticipating the praises of these men to become the catalyst of overcoming Satan's apparent victory. Praise invades Satan's territory and ruins his plans.

Lastly, praise mobilizes God's power. Praise can release God's power into any situation by removing our doubt and expressing our faith and confidence in God. In so doing, we allow God to act to accomplish His will. Although Jesus surely would have liked to have done many things in Capernaum, His hands were tied by their lack of faith. This is why God uses our faith expressed through praise to remove our doubts. In so doing, He removes one major yet subtle barrier to His being able to answer our prayers.

4. On-site Praying

Mid-1989 ushered in the start of a new phenomenon in prayer. Before this, many groups and organizations would have prayer for their meetings. Even conferences would have a limited amount, often restricted to twenty-four-hour prayer chains and/or some staff and participant prayer.

With the convening of Lausanne II in Manila, Philippines, in July of 1989, on-site praying took place by people uninvolved in the conference—people whose sole reason for being at the conference was to provide a twenty-four-hour prayer vigil. This vigil included prayer for the speakers and any problems that arose. Over forty "pray-ers" representing a number of nations were part of the prayer team. The people came from a cross-section of born-again believers from such denominations as Brethren, Baptists, Lutherans, Presbyterians, Anglicans, Assemblies of God, and Foursquare.

With a beautiful spirit of cooperation, the group blended together in prayer. Each one went away with a new appreciation and admiration for those whose style was not quite like theirs. Conference leaders requesting prayer help before speaking felt a special anointing, freedom, and power in their presentations. Since then, there have been several other such successful meetings. During each prayer time the group grew closer, and previous strong barriers melted away. Strong friendships and lasting bonds formed across theological chasms. Even though their respective theologies remained unchanged, their hearts were transformed.

Lausanne became the pattern after which several other major recent conferences were modeled, including a conference for the physically challenged sponsored by Joni Erickson Tada in June of 1990, and InterVarsity's Urbana Mission Conference in December of 1990, which had over twenty thousand in attendance.

So successful were these times of intercessory prayer, so important were their contributions to the success of the conferences, many evangelicals felt that few, if any, important conferences in the future will be held without such on-site prayer covering. Several of those involved in the planning of Urbana reported that prayer was so important that it had permanently changed the complexion of Urbana for the future. Those who were on the receiving end of prayer at both Urbana and Lausanne told the intercessors that they strongly felt the importance, power, and impact of the prayers on their behalf.

Another unique form of on-site praying is that of flagpole praying. This phenomena is most common with youth pastors and youth workers. Meeting quarterly at local high schools, they challenge their youth groups to an early time of prayer around the school's flagpole. They pray for specific educational issues, Christian clubs that meet on campus, outreach events and, as was communicated during the 1992 Los Angeles riots, for protection.

A last on-site praying procedure is spiritual mapping. C. Peter Wagner explains in his *Warfare Prayer:*

> David Barret, who edited the massive *World Christian Encyclopedia,* and who has the most extensive data base for global Christian statistics ever compiled, discerned an area that encompassed North Africa, the Middle East and sections of Asia to Japan. His computer-aided calculations showed that at least 95 percent of the world's unreached peoples and the largest number of non-Christians reside in this area. Luis Bush observed that this area was situated between the latitudes of ten and forty degrees north and drew a rectangle on the map which he calls "The 10/40 Window." This 10/40 window is being widely accepted by missiologists as the most crucial area for the focus of the forces for world evangelization in the 1990s.

This is but one example of spiritual mapping; another is the ability to go into a city and diagram the location of spiritual forces that hinder the work of God so these strongholds can be eliminated. This praying is for concentrated spiritual warfare.

When applied to a local area, much historical research goes into this process. This includes tracing the natives and earliest settlers, understanding the relationships of various peoples, and identifying significant negative events. Specific strongholds of the enemy like pornography shops, drug dealers, prostitution areas, occultic places—such as fortune tellers, New Age bookstores, and cultic or non-Christian places of worship—are also pinpointed.

5. Spiritual Warfare

Most of us don't need to be reminded of Ephesians 6:12; we know that our battle is with spiritual powers. However, a concerted effort has begun to understand and implement prayer strategies in the realm of spiritual warfare. The fast growth of Dr. Neil Anderson's Freedom in Christ Ministries is a clear example of this trend. While the subject of spiritual warfare covers a wide spectrum of views, we feel that in the 1990s more people will become aware of Satan's power and the necessity for training in spiritual warfare.

As 2 Timothy 3:1 reminds us: "There will be terrible times in the last days." The truth of this verse is seen as people turn to a myriad of practices and teachings, hoping to find relief. Unfortunately, many seek answers in experiences like astrology, tarot cards, tea leaves, and the newest medium of crystals and inner guides. Paul warned: "For our struggle is not against flesh and blood, but against the rulers, against the authorities, against the powers of this dark world and against the spiritual forces of evil in the heavenly realms" (Eph. 6:12). This is why we will see a more concerted effort to understand and implement prayer strategies in the realm of spiritual warfare.

To fully comprehend this phenomenon, we need to look at the typical maturing process in the prayer life of a believer. Prayer is not related to age; prayer is related to maturity, knowledge, and practice. So as we look at the figure below, we notice six major levels of prayer for the maturing Christian:

Major Levels of Prayer

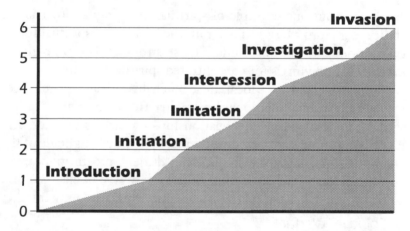

The first level is *Introduction*. After we mature out of our infancy of praying "Now I lay me down to sleep," "God bless the missionaries," and other rote prayers, we realize that we can talk personally to God about those things that concern us. In the Introduction level, people's prayer focus is for their own immediate sphere of interest. Words like "Help me . . ." and "Give me. . ." are plentiful. It is more defensive praying and "I" centered. Seeing answers is very important. Faith is growing, but is very fragile. The key to growth from the Introduction level is practice and burden. This person often prays because he knows he should, not because he has a great desire to. Prayer is irregular, may be dull, and seem like work. To overcome these problems we often challenge the new believer to spend seven minutes with God in an effort to lay a foundation for the higher levels.

The second level is *Initiation*. To initiate prayer growth, the person should move from self-centered praying to a wider scope of requests. Missionaries, crime, drugs, and other social concerns will become part of his prayer focus. He will start claiming appropriate Scriptures for a situation.

As he advances to the third level of *Imitation*, he will be more aware of how others are praying. He may feel comfortable in praying out loud. He senses a greater desire to learn about prayer and may read books and listen to teachings about prayer. Here the foundational elements of modeling become significant. As much may be taught as is caught.

Level number four is *Intercession*. Intercession is defined as prayer offered on behalf of another person as an expression of God's love and concern for the person. Although previously a person may have prayed superficially for God's help for others, intercession becomes a greater burden at this level. As a Christian's relationship with the Lord begins to deepen, so will his prayer life. Prayer will no longer be seen as a dull obligation, but rather a desirable, much-needed part of his life. At this level the person looks forward to seeing God answering prayer, and his increased faith is based on that expectancy. He will become excited as he really sees God at work and becomes much more aware of the power of prayer. He will awaken to a sense of spiritual battles and Satan's activities—creating a desire to thwart the devil's workings.

However, many prayer warriors, new to the arena of intercession, often become overwhelmed by the enormity of the problems they see. Therefore, they tend to be strong at times but may falter when visible results do not come. Because of this flux there are varying levels of intercession. In order for persons to grow in their prayer skills, the fifth level must become their goal.

Investigation is that fifth level. As faith increases, a hunger develops to believe God. At this point, a person reaches out and begins a specific investigation on how to believe for greater things. Added to the foundation already laid is the need to learn more from others about different aspects of prayer. This investigation will come through many resources, such as reading books on prayer and listening to tapes, videos, and radios. In addition, those with a deepening thirst may even attend conferences specifically focused on teaching people more about prayer. As the opportunities increase in the 1990s, some will attend the concerts of prayer and the opportunities to sit under the tutelage of recognized experts in the field of prayer such as Dick Eastman, (President of Change the World Ministries), Evelyn Christianson, (well known speaker and author of *What Happens When Women Pray*), Fuller Seminary Professor C. Peter Wagner, and John Maxwell (senior pastor of Skyline Wesleyan Church in California).

In the local church setting, the investigator may have another friend as a prayer partner. He will participate in prayer opportunities such as prayer meetings and may even be involved in getting others to pray for the Sunday School, the pastor, or be on a prayer chain. At this level, prayer is very exciting to him and his thirst to learn more will be heightened. More time will be spent in prayer, and visible results will be evident—often to the extent of seeing God intervene in direct ways to change situations through specific prayer.

Now before we look at our last level, we need to say that many, if not most, good Christians stop here unless they actively desire to reach a higher level of prayer. And once again, as seen in the imitation level, modeling becomes a key to unlocking the Invasion level.

Our last level is *Invasion*. Here the term "spiritual warfare" is often heard. The person operating at this level is growing in faith and vision. He is willing to defend himself and his loved ones against the attacks of the enemy, as well as going "against the gates of hell." He has a sensitivity to what grieves the Spirit in specific events and particular issues, thus increasing his burden to pray. His joy in praying and seeing God work increases.

As we try to understand this highest level of prayer, never forget that Satan fears no other ministry or event more than prayer. The old hymn states it well, "Satan trembles when he sees the weakest Christian on his knees." Satan can easily concentrate his efforts on unsuspecting people and circumstances, but he cannot stop God's angels from bringing God's answers. With this in mind, the 1990s will see the reclamation of people and territories lost to Satan, through the invasion of God's people in prayer.

Perhaps the 1991 Gulf War offers some keen insights into these strategies in spiritual warfare. Prayer is like the air assault that preceded the ground war. Wave after wave of air strikes bombarded and knocked out the strongholds of the enemy both in communication and physical elements. Without such effective air attacks, the United States inevitably would have had greatly increased losses in the ground war. With these strategic enemy strongholds knocked out or severely crippled, our military was able to launch a successful assault with relatively low incidence of wounding or death. The air assault significantly reduced our casualties and created an atmosphere in which the ground assault was completed in an unheard of one hundred hours. Prior to the air war, not even the greatest optimist envisioned such a low casualty rate. We note with interest that many believers are also convinced that prayer was a significant factor in this low casualty rate and quick victory.

Prayer is even more effective in the war believers face daily. It can go anywhere without hindrance, knock out Satan's strongholds, do significant damage to his plans, and neutralize his ability to launch a successful counterattack. Prayer can help take back from Satan territory he has stolen or long held. When prayer is employed in the right way, more is accomplished for the Lord in a shorter time. In the intensity of the battle, prayer helps defeat Satan and assures believers of ultimate victory.

There are many weapons in the armory of spiritual warfare. For example, Dr. Neil Anderson, with Freedom in Christ Ministries, challenges us to claim the truth of being in Christ when battling the enemy. We need to establish our authority before the enemy, and every Christian is commanded to put on the armor of God. Although we may minimize its importance in the battle, those who understand the dynamics of spiritual warfare realize the crucial value of being properly protected when going into war. What many do not realize, however, is that to be a Christian is to be in a war with the world, the flesh, and Satan. And the degree of daily success in this battle is often contingent upon how well they have prepared for the battle. How well they have listened to their Commander in prayer will set the battle plan for their day. Yet despite a renewed emphasis on prayer, one often neglected element in this preparation is the area of fasting. While some people are not physically able to fast, those who are able can intensify and focus the prayer experience in general. They also can develop a weapon in the upper level of invasion. In the following graph, we have amplified the picture of the sixth level to demonstrate this point.

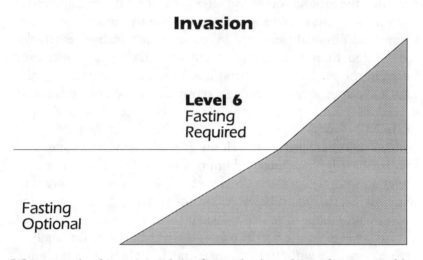

Many involved in spiritual warfare, who have been discouraged by their inability to see the answers they sought, are realizing their answers fall in the area in which fasting is required. Some add this element and are able to make the spiritual breakthrough desired.

6. Prayer Partners

Some churches are organizing key leadership to pray for each other, rotating these partners each quarter. This partnering of people encourages bonding and appreciation for one another. "Triads" seem to work best, with two lay leaders for each staff member in a large church.

Three leaders in a group may work best in medium and smaller churches. Partners pray for their personal walk with the Lord, ministry/work schedules, relationships, and even finances. Once this is in place with key leadership, partnerships are then formed for other leadership such as Sunday School teachers, children's leaders, and so on. Eventually, all leaders in your church should have prayer partners who uphold them before God in prayer.

7. Small-Group Prayer

Older members of your congregation will remember times when churches divided into "cottage" prayer groups. Cottage prayer groups often met for specific concerns, such as a missions conference or evangelistic revival. The dynamic which made these cottage prayer times exciting is still available in small group prayer. Some churches divide into prayer groups to meet in homes once each month. Many use the first Sunday evening of each month for this special purpose. Each person who attends is given the opportunity to share prayer requests and answers to prayers in their own lives. A list of general concerns or requests for the corporate body is usually provided.

8. Prayer Seminars

Prayer seminars can raise the consciousness for prayer and teach people prayer skills. The strength of such seminars is their ability to increase the learning curve of people. Skills that normally take years to acquire may be learned and experienced rapidly in a seminar setting. Growing churches seek to schedule a seminar at least every other year on the basics of prayer, and all church leaders are encouraged to attend. A variety of prayer models and ways to pray are introduced. Prayer seminars include various prayer experiences as well as instruction about prayer.

9. Prayer Retreats

Many people find it difficult to take time to pray in their hectic pace of life. The daily bombardment of media, interruptions, and activities push prayer into the background. So prayer retreats are planned and executed with great impact in churches. When people get away from the everyday routine, they are freed to focus on the still small voice of God. Prayer partners and teams often attend together, and again plenty of time is scheduled for prayer solitude and small-group prayer.

10. Early Morning Prayer

Historically, prayer meetings have been held at various hours of the day. In the first half of this century, prayer meetings developed in the middle of the week and the late evenings. This time proved to be acceptable until our rapid transition into a commuter society. With more people arriving home later in the evening, midweek prayer meeting attendance has declined. Today churches are finding that early morning is a better time to meet than late evenings. A quiet room with soft lighting and quiet background music is often provided, and people are allowed to come and go as they please. Some pray alone while others will group together. Coffee and a light snack are appropriate. A prayer list of church needs is normally given to all who participate.

11. Identification of Intercessors

Historically intercession has been viewed as an attribute and burden of the Lord Jesus Christ. Today we can identify individuals gifted in the area of intercession. Several qualities are apparent in their lives. First is a desire to pray at least an hour per day. Accompanying this motivation is an insatiable yearning to know more, to read more, and to be around models and people with similar focus. This helps to experience the deeper levels of intercession.

These intercessors can be seen in three distinct levels in the growing church: elementary levels, intermediate levels, and advanced levels. The elementary levels are characterized by long-term commitments. They will pray through long lists of concerns and needs. You will find them at your missionary meetings, general prayer meetings, or busily writing down the requests of people from their Sunday School class. The intermediate level are those intercessors who "wait before the Lord." They have a unique sense of the individual needs of people and often provide short-term prayer support in times of crisis. They usually do not have a set agenda for prayer, but rather go to prayer, asking the Lord to show them what He wants them to pray for. The advanced intercessors are the specialists. They may be committed to personal intercession where they provide a prayer covering for individual pastors, leaders, or people groups. Their focus may be geographical where their burden is for a specific city or nation. Some may specialize in topical praying for issues in the government, such as abortion and housing for the homeless. Advanced intercessors will have some of the prayer habits of the elementary and intermediate levels; however, they are much more aggressive in their praying and bolder in their requests. Inevitably, whatever their vision, they will almost always be involved in spiritual warfare.

12. Team Prayer

In past days prayer leadership was primarily modeled through the Sunday worship pastoral prayer time. While this is still a significant model, some churches find that a better way to model prayer is through the pastoral staff and leadership. As church members see their leaders teaming together in prayer, they are encouraged to follow the same pattern. Staff set aside time each day for prayer as a regular part of their quiet time. Once each week the staff prays together for themselves, their church, and requests from the congregation. Each staff member and leader recruits their own prayer team who covers them and their ministry in prayer each day.

Increasing Prayer in Changing Times

In wanting to see our churches grow, we seem to have a choice between two paths. One path is the way of discipline. Here pastors and leaders alike want to make sure they get the job done. So appropriate methods and programs are established to keep the church on track. Updating of skills and employing new insights God gives the church have become priorities to such a leadership. The other path is the way of drifting. Although a unified body may show disciplined programs and vision, it still may be drifting because it floats aimlessly. It takes no effort to drift. But God's power is manifest when a specific course is charted.

Church growth flows from church leadership. Congregations follow the leaders, and prayer is no exception. Jesus modeled prayer to His disciples. Church leaders can pave the way in implementing prayer strategies both in current church activities and in creative, proven practices. This can enhance significant prayer in the church ministry. Evaluate and implement some or all of the following possibilities:

1. Pray

The goal should be to have prayer as foundational to all church ministries. Prayer should be a significant, rather than a cosmetic, agenda item. It should become a natural thing for people to pray about everything—decisions, problems, giving thanks for good things, praying for each other, asking God's blessing and guidance before each ministry activity. Ephesians 6:17 encourages us to do just that.

It may help to have the sanctuary open during office hours for people to come and pray. Or set aside a room specifically designated for prayer. In this room current prayer requests should be available. Also include a topical counseling book for different problems, so those with prayer burdens can look up Scripture for godly wisdom.

31

At the end of services, have trained personnel available to pray with those who come forward.

2. Encourage Significant Staff and Leadership Prayer

If prayer is seen as foundational to all areas of ministry and life, the congregation will know the staff and leadership care about them and are praying for their requests. Have staff set aside time each day for prayer as a regular part of their quiet time. Once weekly have the staff pray together for themselves, the church, and the requests from the congregation.

3. Organize Prayer Partners

Prayer partners provide a prayer covering for key leadership. This will strengthen their relationship and appreciation for each other and create more unity. Have the key leadership, including staff, pray for each other on a rotating basis each quarter. Triads seem to work best with two lay leaders for each staff in a large church, or three leaders in a group for medium and small churches.

Prayer requests—such as for one's personal walk with the Lord, ministry/work schedules, relationships, and finances—can be integrated into this format. Once this is in place with key leadership, a new set of partners can be formed for other leadership such as Sunday School workers and children's ministries personnel.

4. Integrate Prayer into Your Small Groups

Small group prayer provides a place for leadership to model prayer as closer bonding and encouragement is provided. In small groups each person is given the opportunity to share prayer requests and answers to prayers in their own lives. The church can also provide a list of general concerns or requests for the corporate body. Depending upon the needs and the dynamics of the group, prayer can take from ten minutes to half an hour. Small groups may also desire to use a specific book on prayer for their study and discussion. Resources, including tapes on some "how-to's" in this area, are available and listed in the section at the end of this chapter.

5. Include Prayer as an Agenda Item

Prayer on the agenda will generate a heart for seeking God's wisdom and guidance for each meeting time. This will generate unity and oneness of purpose. It also helps to put prayer into its proper place in the structure of the meeting.

Put prayer on the agenda! Suggest that the prayer be focused on the specific areas to be discussed. This will cut down on the wasted time and friction that are often inherent in meetings.

6. Conduct Prayer Seminars

In seminars, training and modeling are provided in a variety of prayer styles. Participants will also experience an expansion of the vision for a prayer ministry.

Schedule a seminar at least every other year on the basics of prayer. Many cities are fortunate to have these activities on a regular basis. Leadership and laity should be encouraged to attend.

7. Hold Leadership Prayer Retreats

These retreats can help leadership see the importance and impact of prayer in their ministry, train them in various styles of prayer, and increase unity and bonding among participants.

Hold weekend prayer retreats with leadership alone or leadership and laity prayer partners. Teaching and modeling of various prayer styles can be added to the extended times of prayer. Such retreats are advisable when major decisions face the church; at such times little teaching is needed. Fasting may be an optional feature.

8. Offer Early Morning Prayer Times

These provide a fresh approach for general prayer partnerships or group praying for a broader number of people in a more relaxed format. This is especially desirable where the traditional prayer meeting is non-existent or poorly attended. Because of the variety, it tends to lessen the guilt often associated with not attending the prayer meeting. Several ways are available: at church for everyone or for an affinity group, on the phone with a partner, or a prayer breakfast on Saturdays.

9. Develop Prayer Opportunities in Sunday School

Train as many as possible in the importance of prayer, increasing their vision, knowledge, and skills.

Offer an adult elective course on prayer. Encourage classes to have prayer for each other's needs. Challenge all Sunday School teachers to get to know the needs of each member and to pray specifically for them. Let the individuals know you are praying for them and get periodic updates. A three-by-five-inch card for each member can help the teacher keep the requests organized.

10. Encourage Leadership to Study Prayer

This broadens the vision, knowledge, and understanding of the intricacies of prayer and gives a greater appreciation of its importance to their particular area of leadership. Start a prayer library. Choose some of the books in the Resources Section for suggested reading. Share at staff or leadership meetings what has been learned and encourage them to share these truths with whom they minister.

A man called his doctor very late one stormy night. Over the phone he said, "Doctor, my wife is very, very sick. Can you come out and help me? You must come over right now." The doctor replied, "I'd love to come over, but my car is in the shop. If you will come and get me, I'll be glad to help." There was silence on the phone for a long time. Then the man was heard to say, "You mean, you want me to come out on a night like this?"

That's exactly what we do with God, isn't it? We want God to do all kinds of incredible things for us while we often neglect to spend serious energy in prayer. The times are changing, but increased prayer will act as both the power supply and the fuel for effective ministry. Those who use it wisely and often will find their God-given goals reached and will be victorious in the spiritual battles they encounter.

▼

RESOURCES

Seminars:

"How to Have a Prayer Ministry in Your Church" and "Releasing the Power of Prayer" conducted by the Charles E. Fuller Institute for Evangelism and Church Growth, P.O. Box 91990,Pasadena, CA 91109-1990; (800) 999-9578.

Tapes:

George, Carl F. *Equipping the Pastor with the Power of Prayer*. Available from the Charles E. Fuller Institute for Evangelism and Church Growth, P.O. Box 91990, Pasadena, CA 91109-1990; (800) 999-9578.

Martin, Dr. Glen S. *Prayer in the 90s: Learning to Apply Prayer Principles*. Available from the Church Growth Network, 3630 Camellia Dr., San Bernardino, CA 92404; (909) 882-5386.

Wagner, Dr. C. Peter *How to Have a Prayer Ministry*. Available from the Charles E. Fuller Institute for Evangelism and Church Growth, P.O. Box 91990, Pasadena, CA 91109-1990; (800) 999-9578.

Newsletters:

The Breakthrough Intercessor. Available from Breakthrough, Inc., Lincoln, VA 22078.

For Further Reading:

Aldrich, Joseph. *Prayer Summits* (Portland, Oreg.: Multnomah Press, 1992).

Bell, Steve and Mains, David. *Two Are Better Than One* (Portland, Oreg.: Multnomah Press, 1991).

Bright, Bill and Jennings, Ben. *Unleashing the Power of Prayer* (Chicago: Moody Press, 1989).

Bryant, David. *Concerts of Prayer* (Ventura, Calif.: Gospel Light Inc./Regal Books, 1984).

Dawson, John. *Taking Our Cities for God: How to Break Spiritual Strongholds* (Lake Mary, Fla.: Creation House, 1989).

Duewel, Wesley L. *Touch the World Through Prayer*. (Grand Rapids, Mich.: Zondervan, 1986).

Duewel, Wesley L. *Mighty Prevailing Prayer* (Grand Rapids, Mich.: Zondervan, 1990).

Gentle, Ernest. *Awaken the Dawn* (Portland, Oreg.: Bible Temple Pub., 1990).

Jacobs, Cindy. *Possessing the Gates of the Enemy* (Grand Rapids, Mich.: Chosen Books, 1991).

Otis, George. *The Last of the Giants* (Grand Rapids, Mich.: Chosen Books, 1991).

Sherrer, Quin. *How to Pray for Your Family and Friends* (Ann Arbor, Mich.: Servant Publications, 1990).

Wagner, C. Peter. (ed.) *Engaging the Enemy* (Ventura, Calif.: Regal Books, 1991).

Wagner, C. Peter. *Warfare Prayer* (Ventura, Calif.: Regal Books, 1992).

Wagner, C. Peter. *Prayer Shield.* (Ventura, Calif.: Regal Books, 1992).

Wagner, C. Peter. *Breaking Strongholds in Your City* (Ventura, Calif.: Regal Books, 1993).

3

Even if you're on the right track,
you'll get run over if you just stand still.
—Will Rogers

When you're through changing, you're through.
—Unknown

WORSHIP

A researcher in Switzerland, long the bastion of watchmaking excellence and profits, discovered a way to use the vibrating frequency of a piece of quartz crystal to keep incredibly accurate time. When presented to the decision makers of the company, they looked hard for all of the familiar components of past success.

"Of what is the main spring made?" they queried. "Where are the twenty-three jeweled parts that have set the world's time-keeping standard? Where is the stem to wind the watch or to adjust the time?"

This new watch did not fit their rigid expectations of what a watch should be, so they rejected it as an idea that would never catch on.

After the Japanese started mass producing the very watch the Swiss rejected, Swiss market share dropped from near 80 percent to 10 percent. The inability to view the world as it could be instead of as it always has been was indeed costly.[1]

Worship is changing today as much as watches have changed. Some churches are taking advantage of the new opportunities for creating new worship styles. Others seem to ignore the new trends. Unable to view worship in a new light, some churches are stuck in a older form of worship which attracts fewer and fewer worshipers.

Haddon Robinson pointed out this change when he said,

> We live in a day where communication is dominated by television. It is a post-literate age. We are now an oral, musical, visual culture. The use of the narrative story is primary.
>
> Gone is the world of Greco-Roman rhetoric (proposition and 3 arguments). People in our culture know nothing of the Bible, don't take church seriously, and are anti-moral. We must be mission-minded, not professional.[2]

Worship

That was then...	This is now...
▲ Hymns	▲ Praise songs
▲ Organ/piano	▲ Small band
▲ Hymn books	▲ Overheads/slides
▲ Song leader	▲ Worship leader
▲ Slower pacing	▲ Faster pacing
▲ Quietness	▲ Talking
▲ Softer sounds	▲ Louder sounds
▲ Longer service	▲ Shorter service
▲ Sermon	▲ Message
▲ Standard format	▲ Variable format
▲ Bulletin	▲ Worship folder
▲ Soft lighting	▲ Bright lighting
▲ Contemplative atmosphere	▲ Celebrative atmosphere
▲ Choir	▲ Praise team
▲ Content-oriented	▲ Heart-oriented
▲ Sanctuary	▲ Auditorium
▲ Audio orientation	▲ Visual orientation
▲ Varied talent used	▲ Best talent used
▲ Haphazard service	▲ Rehearsed service
▲ Little planning	▲ Much planning

Worship Trends

A joke occasionally heard among pastors is that when Satan fell from heaven he landed in the choir loft. And, true to his character, he has made the most trouble for churches through music and worship ever since. Some church leaders add that it would be easier to add a fourth person to the Trinity than to change hymn books.

We are keenly aware of the emotional attachment people have to particular styles of worship. No other character of a church so clearly defines its identity and philosophy of ministry. However, the times are changing even in worship styles, and effective churches will take note of them. Here are a few trends we've observed in the area of worship.

1. Desire to Meet with God

The Reformation and the Great Awakening had an impact upon corporate worship in two distinct ways. Highlighting the need for right thinking, the Reformation influenced worship by focusing on the "content" of worship. The emphasis on knowledge or doctrine led to a more restrained worship style. In contrast, highlighting the need to experience God, the Great Awakening focused on the "feelings" of worship. The emphasis on experiencing God, His power, and personal touch resulted in a more emotional style of worship.

No one could miss the fact that worship is in a transitional phase. Today churches seek worship which is balanced between "content" and "feelings." We like to say that churches today want worship that is both head-oriented and heart-oriented, where worshipers can learn about God and meet with God and sing about God and sing to God.

2. Seeker-sensitive Services

Church consultants are fond of asking the question "Who is your client?" Churches typically offer only two answers: "Our client is the Christian" or "Our client is the unbeliever." And the past ten years have seen growth in the number of churches which give the second answer.

These churches are typically described as either "seeker-centered" or "seeker-sensitive." Seeker-centered churches usually are new church plants which have chosen to target almost exclusively the unchurched. Seeker-sensitive churches include older and newer congregations which have chosen to use a worship style more user-friendly to the unchurched, but not exclusively targeted toward them.

One of the most visible aspects of these seeker churches is the renaming of traditional church concepts to be understandable to the unchurched. Here are a few we've discovered. You may be able to think of many more new names for old things:

▲ program instead of bulletin

▲ guests instead of visitors

▲ auditorium instead of sanctuary

▲ lobby instead of narthex

▲ application instead of content

▲ truth instead of doctrine

▲ principle instead of dogma

▲ practice instead of tradition

3. Festival Worship Atmosphere

Speaking of the Macintosh Computer team, Apple CEO John Sculley writes in *Odyssey:* "The Mac team thought of the product every minute they were awake. They often worked through the night, foregoing sleep in a creative frenzy to resolve a technical enigma. When I would visit them, their hair was often mussed, their faces often creased with sleepiness, but their eyes always seemed to glisten with excitement."[3]

In a similar way, spirit lives in certain churches. You can see it in the way people act. You can hear it in their singing. You can feel it in the atmosphere.

Worship services that are attracting people in our changing times have a festival atmosphere rather than an oppressive one. The general term for this festive feeling is "celebrative worship." Clearly defining a celebrative worship service is difficult, yet we all seem to know one when we are in one. From a practical point of view, worship is celebrative when:

▲ People attend—Celebrative services attract people who come because they want to rather than because they have to.

▲ People bring friends—Celebrative services not only attract people but they also cause worshipers to bring their friends.

▲ People participate—Celebrative services create an environment where singing, giving, praying, and other areas of worship are entered into with enthusiasm.

▲ People listen—Celebrative services hold the attention of worshipers throughout the entire time of worship.

▲ People grow—Celebrative services challenge individuals to make biblical decisions that affect their daily living.

This move toward a festival atmosphere is seen in the use of small bands playing contemporary music, paced in a faster tempo than hymns. It is seen in the change from a contemplative quietness in a softly lit sanctuary to a lively talking together in a brightly lit auditorium before the service. It is seen in the participative clapping and hugging, as contrasted to the sedate and attentive rigidness of older worship styles.

4. Emphasis on Quality

Most of us can remember a time when "Made in Japan" meant poor quality and "Made in the USA" stood for the highest quality. We may also be able to remember when "church" stood for a higher quality than that found in the world in general. For example, in years gone by, where would you have likely found the most educated people, the best public speakers, the top musicians, the superior music, the finest art? The answer in many cases was the church.

Some, of course, would argue that American products rank with the best. But the buying habits of consumers over the past twenty years certainly illustrate that poor quality standards are unacceptable to the buying public. The availability of direct communication via radio, television, video, and compact discs makes it possible for nearly every person to be exposed to the best products or experiences available. People feel they deserve quality, and they want it.

This demand for higher quality was brought home to us a few years ago when a denominational executive shared that a small congregation of twenty-nine people located in an extremely rural community had lost their pastor. One of the church leaders had called our friend to give him a list of the church's requirements for a new pastoral candidate. Among the requirements were such items as (1) fluent in Greek and Hebrew, (2) experienced worship leader, and (3) superb communication skills. Tough requirements for the pastor of a church of twenty-nine people!

As we discussed this, our friend commented, "I don't have any place to hide my poor pastors any more." He explained that in former years a small, rural church would be pleased to take any pastor who would simply love them. However, with the advent of television, even people in small, rural churches have been exposed to the planned worship services, excellent messages, and superior music of some of the best churches in the United States. They no longer wish to accept anything but the highest quality.

It is no longer easy for churches to ignore the quality control issue. The trend among growing churches is for well-planned, rehearsed worship services using the best in musicians, sound equipment, and communication skills.

5. Use of the Arts

An increased understanding of the nature of spiritual gifts in the 1970s led to a broader acceptance of people's talents in all areas. Even though the church at large has always been a haven and sponsor for art, crafts, and plays, for the most part such expression by gifted people is just beginning to be understood and highlighted by congregations.

An excellent example of the use of the arts for church growth is seen in Victoria Community Church in Riverside, California. An independent church of approximately 150 worshipers associated with the Christian & Missionary Alliance, this congregation called a new pastor gifted in the writing and production of full-length plays. Over an eleven-year period the church placed an emphasis on developing a complete drama and music ministry which involved people from inside and outside the congregation as artists, actors and actresses, set builders, sound and lighting technicians, and directors. During this eleven-year period the church grew to two thousand worshipers meeting in two services on Sunday morning.

A visible trend involves the use of five-minute dramas[4] as introductions and conclusions to sermons, music centers for voice and instrumental training (for the church and the community) and, although not acceptable in most churches, interpretive dance.

6. Relational-styled Worship

Generally speaking, our society has not been good for relationships. The mobility of people has torn apart the natural networks of family, friends, and neighbors. Working farther away from home has created a commuter society where people hold essentially two jobs—their work and driving twenty hours weekly to it. Exposure to too many people, too much information, and too many expectations leads to people resisting relationships even when they want them.

The Christian life, of course, is built on relationships: a vertical relationship with God and a horizontal relationship with people (see 1 John 1:3). In response to the need for healthier relationships, churches are designing relational-styled worship services.

The change in church architecture is a good example of how relationships are shaping worship. Originally, church auditoriums were built with straight pews stretching directly back from the platform. People in the rear of the auditorium usually had difficulty in seeing the faces of the people on the platform, and all they saw of other worshipers was the back of each other's head. Today newer churches take advantage of the growing desire for relational worship by using semicircular seating where people are able to see each other's faces and the audience is brought closer to the platform.

Another aspect of relational worship is the use of worship leaders rather than song directors and worship teams rather than choirs. The song leader used to be a master of ceremonies of sort during the worship service. Choirs stood far away from the audience and sang anthems beyond the singing ability of most people in the pew. In contrast, today's worship leader guides the congregation into a relationship with God through the skilled use of music, prayer, words, and timing. The worship team stands close to the congregation, often singing simpler songs in unison with them.

Increasing Worship in Changing Times

Pastor Rick Warren of Saddleback Community Church in Mission Viejo, California, says that "Advertising will bring people to your church one time, but it will not bring them back unless you can deliver the goods."[5] The "goods" that newcomers first notice is the worship service atmosphere and all the surrounding amenities such as child care, friendliness of people, adequate parking, and seating. It is a fact of church life that no one joins a church without attending the worship service. Hence, it is crucial to have a dynamic worship service as the center post of everything else a church does.

1. Plan a Dynamic Worship Service

Look at any recent study on why people do not attend church and you will find that people think church worship services are boring. Today's information-rich society bombards people with constant images, sales pitches, and other visual stimuli to keep their attention. Then, when people visit a church they typically find a slowly paced service with little visual appeal. Confronted with a lack of stimulus, their minds begin to wander, leading to feelings of boredom.

People who feel worship services are boring do not mean that God is boring nor do they mean the Bible is boring. What they mean is the pace of the service is boring. Today's effective church seeks to hold people's attention by developing a dynamic worship service. As one writer says, "The pastors are the artistic overseers of worship. They must be creative, combining the elements of mood, sound, timing, and energy to create an atmosphere where worship can happen. The aim is to capture the attention and hopefully the imagination, to turn people's minds to God."[6]

Build around one theme. Celebrative worship services have a sense of unity that is best achieved by building the entire service around one basic theme. Identify the broad theme you wish to communicate to your audience. Select and use music that fits your theme. Be sure to relate your introductions, transitional comments, and even your announcements to the theme.

Plan for participation. Celebrative worship services keep people alert by involving them in meaningful ways throughout the service. Allow people to participate by singing, clapping, standing, shaking hands, filling in blanks in a study guide, praying, hugging, talking, laughing, crying, etc.

Develop a sense of flow. Celebrative worship services lead people along so that they sense a clear flow or progression in the service. Think through how each part of the service relates to the whole. Remember: sporadic or disconnected components will cause people to become distracted and disinterested.

Speed up the pace. Celebrative worship services move quickly enough to keep people's attention focused on the service. Speed up the pace of your worship service by singing and playing music faster. Vary the pace by using upbeat tempos and slower reflective tempos to keep people's attention.

Eliminate dead time. Celebrative worship services move quickly between parts of the services, allowing for little dead time where people may lose their attentiveness. To enhance your worship service develop good transitions between its various elements. All movement between people and elements of worship should take place quickly and smoothly.

Use variety. Celebrative worship services use a variety of worship elements to maintain everyone's interest and enjoyment. Include elements such as drama, interviews, video, a message, the greeting of one another, Scripture reading, an offering and music.

2. Recruit a Worship Team

Worship teams are a key to developing a celebrative worship service as they spread the responsibility among several people and, most importantly, use the creativity of several people rather than only one. A complete worship team will include at least the following people or roles.

The Senior Pastor. The senior pastor must own the worship service and play a major role in its development. As the main speaker at the worship service, the pastor must prepare messages well in advance and be able to present the theme of each service at least eight weeks before the actual service. This will allow the worship team ample time to plan a dynamic service.

Worship Leader. Someone other than the pastor should lead the worship team. This person needs to be a "people" person, with sound musical ability and solid platform presence. Most of all, this person must be able to lead the corporate congregation in worship.

Communication/Coordination Director. The pastor and worship leader need not be responsible for contacting all the parties involved in the worship service. Instead, someone with excellent organizational ability should be involved to pull everything together. The communication director takes responsibility for contacting the ushers, greeters, musicians, parking attendants, and others who may be involved in the service.

In smaller churches these three parties will be the entire worship team. Larger churches will need to expand their worship team by adding at least two additional people.

Drama Coordinator. The drama coordinator is responsible for recruiting, training, planning, and producing dramas during the worship services.

Sound and Lighting Technician. This person takes responsibility for coordinating the sound and lights.

The worship team meets weekly to do three things. First, they pray together for the worship services. Second, each week they evaluate the past week's worship service. Third, they plan for future worship services.

Churches wanting to have the very best worship services schedule a weekly rehearsal or walk-through of the service prior to Sunday morning, or at least early on Sunday morning. Room is left for spontaneity, but most successful worship teams find that practice helps create celebrative services. The more complex the worship service, the greater the need for rehearsal.

3. Begin a Talent Development Process

With the time crunch on our hectic life-styles, some churches find that evening worship services are not as effective as they once were. As a result, churches sometimes either eliminate Sunday evening worship services entirely or restructure them into small groups, Bible studies, or family events.

One of the great advantages of evening worship services over the years was the opportunity for people to practice. Children, youth, and adults found the evening service a good place to practice singing, playing the piano and organ, leading worship, giving announcements, ushering, greeting, and even preaching.

With the gradual demise of the traditional evening worship service, this opportunity to practice and learn has become a missing ingredient in some churches. In many churches it was a tradition to have the youth group lead the entire evening worship service on a regular basis. This was excellent training for future church leaders. Where do people practice and learn the skills necessary for leading Sunday morning worship?

To fill in this training gap, we suggest that churches begin a talent development process by doing three things.

First, eliminate permanent volunteer positions. Everyone who has served in a church remembers the lady who played the organ and, in reality, practically owned it. She would lock the organ following the service and take the key home with her! If new people who could play the organ began attending church, they usually never had the opportunity to use their gift because the organ player held a permanent position. By eliminating such permanent positions and rotating the playing of instruments between several talented people, a church accomplishes several important aspects of ministry: more people use their God-given talents and gifts, and new people are prepared and trained for future ministry. This will be crucial when a church adds a second or third worship service.

Second, begin offering music lessons. The loss of tax revenue to public schools has caused some to eliminate programs not considered core courses. Among those programs eliminated or greatly reduced have been choral and instrumental music. The net effect has been a generation lacking the skills needed to contribute to some areas of worship, especially the music areas. This is one of the reasons for the disinterest in choral music and the inability of the younger generation to read music. In many instances they just haven't had the training.

Creative churches take advantage of this vacuum by offering lessons in music (voice, choral, and instrumental) and in drama. Lessons offered to those outside the church provide an evangelism event as an entry point for the gospel. Lessons offered to people within the church provide a means of discipleship and spiritual gift development. In both cases, new leadership is trained for future ministry.

Third, create forum opportunities. With the demise of the traditional evening worship service, there is a need to create forums for people to practice their music, drama, and speaking talents. One forum which flows naturally out of lessons is the recital. Another forum is a choir or music performance given once or twice a year. Still another forum is a full-length play.

These forums tend to be of higher quality than the traditional Sunday School program put on by many churches at Christmas and Easter. They are well-produced, excellent presentations. Of course, they are advertised to the general public and serve the additional purpose of outreach.

4. Communicate Visually

An interesting difference among the last three generations born in the United States is the contrast in audio and visual orientation. The generation born prior to 1950 read books, played games, and listened to the radio. They were and are a generation that knows how to sit quietly and listen. The next two generations, popularly known as baby boomers and baby busters, were the first generations to be raised with the visual exposure of television and video. They are visually oriented, and the signs indicate that the next generation will be even more tied to visual mediums.

Churches effectively reaching these younger generations take seriously the need to communicate visually. In a simple format, the popular use of overhead projectors for teaching and singing is an example of the effectiveness of visual communication.

Community Baptist Church in Manhattan Beach, California, hired a pastor to work part time producing videos to give announcements, promote church events, and introduce the church to visitors. Instead of following up guests in their homes, guests are given a fifteen-minute video which introduces the church to them. Guests can view the video in their own home, on their own schedule, and without the need to entertain visitors from the church.

5. Preach Practical Messages

The flickering images hit the airwaves on April 30, 1939. President Franklin D. Roosevelt gave a short speech declaring open the New York World's Fair. It was the first public broadcast of an electronic medium called television.

In the fifty-plus years since its formal debut, television has emerged not only as a primary entertainment medium but as a major force for social and cultural change. Here are some ways that television has influenced people as well as some ideas on how to communicate to today's audience.

Immediate Satisfaction. Products are sold, complex issues are solved, and victory is won within thirty minutes on television. The ideas of delayed gratification and a process of spiritual growth are not well accepted. People want patience, and they want it now!

To communicate to people who want immediate satisfaction, preach character sketches of biblical people, pointing out the process each took to mature in their faith. Share real-life examples of people who waited for prayers to be answered, for personal problems to be solved, and for personal growth to occur.

Increased Boredom. Television gives the impression that life moves at a faster pace than it actually does. People subconsciously compare the real world with the fast-paced, action-oriented pulse of a television series. Life seems slow and mundane in comparison.

To communicate to people who are increasingly bored, speed up the pace of worship services and preach sermons no longer than thirty minutes. Get to your point quickly by making your applications the main points of your message.

Short Attention Span. Television commercials have created short attention spans. Chase scenes and rapidly changing action shots have created a climate where people tend to concentrate for only about thirty seconds. Half-hour programs are divided into a series of ten-minute segments, allowing viewers to use the rest room or raid the refrigerator at precise intervals.

To communicate to people with short attention spans, learn to preach without notes and to move away from the pulpit. Vary volume, pitch, and pace of delivery. Organize messages into blocks of seven minutes each, and make a major change for each block.

Personal Touch. Relational aspects of communication are up, and transfer of content is down. Letter writing is diminishing with the phone call and fax machine taking its place. The motto "Reach Out and Touch Someone" typifies this fundamental change in the area of communication. To communicate to people who need a personal touch, deliver sermons from the floor, close to the people, rather than from the platform, removed from the people. Communicate the points of sermons in one-to-one fashion by telling stories that touch the lives of people.

Multiple Story Lines. We no longer live in a sequential world. Television weaves two or three story lines into a thirty-minute episode. People carry on many activities and lines of thought at the same time.

To communicate to people used to multiple story lines, try weaving two story lines into one message. Tell two personal stories, one from the Bible and one from a person living today.

In-and-Out Mentality. Television has taught us that we can step into an episode, and it will stand alone. Sitcoms such as the popular series "Cheers" carried us along with regular characters, but each episode was a complete story in and of itself. Viewers could drop in at any time and understand what was going on.

To communicate to people who have an in-and-out mentality, keep your sermons short and never use a "to be continued" ending. Make sure each sermon stands alone as a complete unit.

We may not like what television has done to the ability of people to sit and listen to our sermons, but to deny and ignore the changes will lead to an empty auditorium. We may be preaching fine sermons, but fewer people will be there to hear them.

Life-cycles of Worship: Two Models

A celebrative worship service takes more than excellent music, committed people, and a fine sermon. It takes solid understanding of how to use the cycles of energy throughout a worship service to create flow and movement. The many types of worship services fall into two basic styles: traditional and contemporary. Either can be celebrative if proper use is made of the emerging cycles of energy.

Life-cycle of a Traditional Service

Traditional worship services seek to move people through three cycles of energy. Each cycle moves increasingly higher in energy use and allows the worshiper to rest briefly following each movement in preparation for the next surge upward.

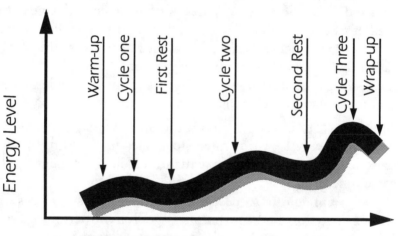

This movement can be expressed as follows:

Warm-up: People arrive for the worship service and are given an opportunity to warm up by greeting others, listening to a prelude, and quietly preparing their hearts for worship.

Cycle one: A hymn of praise begins the formal service leading up to the reading of Scripture which brings the Word of God to the people.

First rest: Announcements are given to communicate information and, most importantly, allow the worshipers to experience a time of rest in preparation for the second cycle.

Cycle two: A hymn of confession leads the congregation to the pastoral prayer which presents their needs to God.

Second rest: An offering is taken as an act of worship, but in terms of movement and flow gives the congregation another brief rest before the third and final cycle takes place.

Cycle three: A choir anthem or special music presentation prepares the way for the pastor's message to the congregation. This third cycle challenges the worshipers to change their lives based on the principles of God's Word.

Wrap-up: Following the final cycle and challenge from God's Word, the worshipers sing a final song of commitment and leave the service at a higher energy level than at the beginning of the service.

Life-cycle of a Contemporary Service

Contemporary services also seek to move people through cycles of energy and rest but appear to have only two cycles. However, the first cycle may actually contain several cycles of energy and rest.

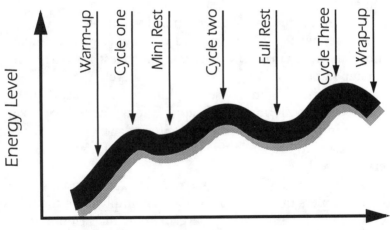

This movement can be expressed as follows:

Warm-up: People arrive for the worship service and are given opportunity to warm up by listening to upbeat contemporary music played by a live band or contemporary music tapes or compact discs played through an excellent sound system. Worshipers focus on their relationships through a wide variety of means which often includes loud talking.

Cycle one: The worship leader and team leads the congregation in a series of four to six upbeat contemporary songs selected to get worshipers participating in the service through clapping and singing. People are encouraged to greet each other while the live band continues playing and the congregation moves in and out of each song with little to no interruption. A personal welcome is given to the congregation within the flow of the music.

Mini rest: With no break, the worship leader begins to guide the congregation into a mini rest of slower paced songs selected to focus the worshipers' minds and hearts on God. Prayer is a vital aspect of this part of the cycle which allows the worshipers to rest in preparation for the rest of the service.

Cycle two: This is in reality a continuance of the first cycle since no full break may actually take place. The worship leader may lead the congregation in a full cycle of nearly twenty to thirty minutes of worship. Following the mini rest noted above, the worship leader gradually returns the people toward a more upbeat tempo by selecting songs which focus on the believers' relationship with each other.

Full rest: At the end of this extended period of worship, a break takes place where an offering and communication of important information is shared. This allows people to rest after the extended worship in preparation for the second full cycle.

Cycle three: This final cycle is highlighted by a practical message from the Bible offering specific applications which the worshipers can put into practice immediately. Stories and illustrations bring the message to life while providing models of how the Scripture relates to real life.

Wrap-up: Following the practical message from God's Word, the worshipers may sing a final song or simply leave the worship service with a higher energy level than at the beginning of the service. The live band continues to play as the people leave, or music may be played through the sound system.

Whatever style of worship a church chooses to use, for it to be celebrative, attention must be given to guiding the worshipers through the cycles of energy and rest, gradually raising the energy level from low to high. With good planning, skilled worship leaders are able to accomplish this with a touch of spontaneity and sensitivity to the movement of the Holy Spirit in the worship service.

Walk into some worship services and sense the enthusiasm in the air. It is hard to define this feeling, yet we instinctively know celebrative worship services have it and others do not. While we certainly don't want to create a false enthusiasm, if worshipers experience high energy, they will likely view the service as celebrative. If the energy level is low, they may never return.

Church leaders sometimes say, "We don't want to entertain people." In reality what they mean is, "We don't want to amuse people." *Amusement* means to "idle away time; to divert attention." *Entertainment* means to "hold the attention of." Worship services should not amuse, but they *should* hold the attention of worshipers. Celebrative worship services take seriously the mental, spiritual, relational, and emotional nature of the worshipers and include all these aspects in a strategy to properly "entertain" them.

▼

NOTES

[1] Larry A. Schmalback, "How Do You View the World?" *The Light* (September–October 1991), 1-2.

[2] Haddon Robinson, "Preaching Has to Change . . .," *Lifelong Learning 1*, No. 5 (October 1990), 1.

[3] Quoted by Duncan Maxwell, Anderson and Richard Poe in "A Culture of Achievement" *Leadership* (June 1992), 31.

[4] Willow Creek Community Church is a pioneer in the use of short dramas. See the resource section for information to order these dramas.

[5] Rick Warren, *The Saddleback Church Growth Manual* (Mission Viejo, Calif.: Saddleback Valley Community Church, 1991), 4.

[6] Lin Yaeger Sexton, "The Sermon You Don't Know You're Preaching," *Leadership* (Carol Stream, Ill.: Spring 1983), 55.

RESOURCES

Seminars:

Artists in Christian Testimony (ACTS). Rev. Byron Spradlin offers seminars and individual consultation on worship and church growth. Write 9521 "A" Business Center Dr., Rancho Cucamonga, CA 91730 or call (714) 987-3274.

Webber, Robert E. *Principles of Worship.* A three-hour video series adapts the concepts of Webber's *Worship Is a Verb* for classes, retreats, and continuing education. Available from Worship Resources, Inc. , 1989, 219 W. Franklin, Wheaton, IL 60187; (708) 665-2895.

Magazines, newsletters, and journals:

CCM Magazine. The authoritative mouthpiece of Christian contemporary music. Write P.O. Box 2070, Knoxville, IA 50197-2070; (800) 333-9643.

Media & Values. A quarterly publication of the Center for Media & Values. A non-profit organization offering research and resources about the influence of media on society. Seminars, workshops, and publications available. Write 1962 S. Shenandoah, Los Angeles, CA 90034 or call (213) 559-2944.

Youthworker. Fall 1991 issue on "The Media." *Youthworker* Subscription Service, P.O. Box 17017, North Hollywood, CA 91615; (818) 760-8983.

Leadership. Spring 1986 (465 Gundersen Dr., Carol Stream, IL 60188). The entire issue is dedicated to the topic of worship.

Drama:

Meriwether Publishing Ltd., P.O. Box 7710, Colorado Springs, CO 80933; (719) 594-4422. Request catalog related to Christian drama and church-related scripts.

Lamb's Players Hennepin Present Developing a Drama Group: A Practical Approach for Director, Actor, and Designer. Also, *Fifteen Surefire Scripts.* Available from World Wide Publications, 1303 Hennepin Ave., Minneapolis, MN 55409; (612) 333-0940.

Sunday Morning Live. Drama sketches, scripts, and illustrative videos available from Willow Creek Resources. Ask for catalog from Zondervan Direct Source, 5300 Patterson SE, Grand Rapids, MI 49502-1292; (800) 876-7335.

For Further Reading:

Allen, Ronald B., and Borror, Gordon. *Worship: Rediscovering the Missing Jewel.* Portland, Oreg.: Multnomah Press, 1987.

Berkley, James D. *Word and Worship.* Vol. 1 of the Leadership Handbooks of Practical Theology. Grand Rapids, Mich.: Baker Book House, 1992.

Coleman, Michael, and Lindquist, Ed. *Come and Worship.* Old Tappan, N.J.: Chosen Books/Fleming H. Revell, 1989.

Hunt, T. W. *Music in Missions: Discipling Through Music.* Nashville: Broadman Press, 1987.

Liesch, Barry. *People in the Presence of God.* Grand Rapids, Mich.: Zondervan, 1988.

Patterson, Ben. *The Grand Essentials.* Waco, Tex.: Word, 1989.

Wardle, Terry Howard. *Exhalt Him! Designing Dynamic Worship Services.* Camp Hill, Penn.: Christian Publications, 1988.

Webber, Robert E. *Worship Is a Verb.* Waco, Tex.: Word, 1983.

Willimon, William H. *Preaching and Leading Worship.* Philadelphia: The Westminster Press, 1984.

4

*Survey Shows Pastors Are Among
Most Occupationally Frustrated*
— Title of article in the *Christian Times*

*Failure to take risks doesn't prevent failure—
it just turns life into slow death.*
— Unknown

LEADERSHIP

Off the coast of Maine lies an island so small that the surrounding ocean can be seen from any point on the island. A visitor started a Sunday School class on the island and gathered the children for their first lesson. "How many of you," he asked, "have ever seen the Atlantic Ocean?" To his surprise, not a single hand went up. The children had, of course, seen the ocean, but it was so much a part of their environment that they simply took it for granted.[1]

There is such a thing as being so much a part of one's environment that we're simply not aware of it. It's the old story of not seeing the forest for the trees. Father John Colbein said we don't know for sure who discovered water, but we're pretty sure it wasn't the fish. Those Sunday School children saw the water—they just didn't know it was the Atlantic Ocean. If they'd had a chance to sail on it or fly across it, they would have had a deeper appreciation for it. And so with all of us. Whatever our present vision is, it is limited. It needs extension.

The Bible says that where there is no vision, the people perish. Our vision shapes us. Our vision controls us. Our vision determines who and what we become. Our vision of how we want to look determines the clothing we buy, the hairstyle we have, and the accessories we wear. Our vision of what a family is determines what our family life is like. Our vision of what a marriage is determines what our marriage becomes.

Likewise, vision shapes our leadership. The first Christians were moved by a vision from Christ to "make disciples of all the nations." Throughout history, people who could communicate God's vision for a particular time and place were leaders whom others were willing to follow. John Wesley once declared "Give me a hundred men who love nothing but God and hate nothing but sin, and I will shake the whole world for Christ."[2] Now that's a vision. Zig Ziglar puts it succinctly: "One person with conviction is worth more than one hundred with only interest."

Leadership

That was then...	This is now...
▲ Staff care	▲ Lay care
▲ Reactive	▲ Proactive
▲ Lower expectations	▲ Higher expectations
▲ Single leadership style	▲ Adaptive leadership style
▲ Enabler	▲ Equipper
▲ Evaluated by knowledge	▲ Evaluated by effectiveness
▲ Fear the future	▲ Create the future
▲ Care taker	▲ Risk taker
▲ Keeps information	▲ Communicates information
▲ Tell people how to do it	▲ Tell people what to do
▲ Others set the pace	▲ Leader sets the pace
▲ A boss	▲ A mentor
▲ "Lone Ranger"	▲ Team player
▲ Leadership demanded	▲ Leadership earned
▲ Based on age	▲ Based on gifts
▲ Dictator	▲ Mentor

Leadership Trends

Leadership is not found in position; it is found in action and influence. People are not looking for managers. Who ever heard of a world manager? World leader . . . yes. Educational leader, political leader, community leader, religious leader . . . yes. People want to be led. The qualifications for leadership have not changed all that much, but many of the styles and criteria have changed.

1. Mentoring Disciples

Webster defines a mentor as "a trusted counselor or guide." A mentor guides or models the attributes and attitudes necessary for success in any given area.

A mentor must model:

▲ the difference between leadership and management. Leaders share their lives; managers do their job. The apostle Paul wrote about this kind of loving leadership in 1 Thessalonians 2:8, "Having thus a fond affection for you, we were well pleased to impart to you not only the gospel of God but also our own lives, because you had become very dear to us" (NASB). If we engage in ministry we may get tired "in" the work of the Lord, but if all we do is immerse ourselves in activity we may get tired "of" the work of the Lord.

▲ the difference between popularity and success. In 1974 Bill Cook wrote a book titled *Success, Motivation and the Scriptures.* Here are his opening remarks:

Someone better tie success and the spiritual together.

Success salesmen aren't carrying the day. They are well aware they reach only a small percentage of the market. And of that percentage, only a few really succeed.

Christians aren't carrying the day either. The percentage of the world population considered thrilling, well-adjusted, achieving Christians is not very large at all.

The rest of the world sits off skeptically observing. That percentage (probably more than half of the people) won't buy success principles which fail to relate to the spiritual side of life, and they want nothing to do with a Christianity that can't tell them how to be successful.[3]

Mentors remind us that there are no small people in the eyes of God. That means leaders stay at the back of the line until God moves them to the front.

▲ the difference between responding and reacting. Animals react. Leaders respond. Step on the tail of a cat and see how quickly it reacts. Professionals demonstrate leadership, not dictator-

59

ship. Under pressure, dictators tend to overreact to a situation. Try to push a piece of string. It will not take much pushing before the string folds up. When pulled, it will move in an orderly manner. A leader goes before the people modeling a proper response to pressure, frustration, and hindrances.

▲ the difference between pain and joy. For the first couple of years in a ministry, leaders experience joy, often called the honeymoon. About year three, they typically encounter the pain of leadership as the result of changes introduced in the first two years. A leader models balance between pain and joy. Ministry brings self-awareness; we find out all that we are not, and loneliness results. It is then God begins to work on us as leaders. Leaders know the experience of Lamentations 3:25–28, "The Lord is good to those whose hope is in him, to the one who seeks him; it is good to wait quietly for the salvation of the Lord. It is good for a man to bear the yoke while he is young. Let him sit alone in silence, for the Lord has laid it on him."

2. Adaptive Leadership Style

Studies have attempted to identify the "right" leadership style to run an organization. Two common threads identified are a concern for people and a concern for tasks. Blake and Mouton created the grid shown below to help understand this approach.[4]

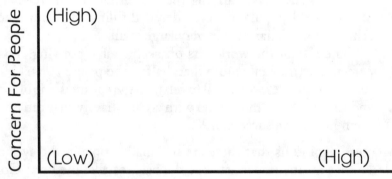

Leadership Style

Recent studies have concluded that categorizing leadership behavior is not this simple. Often the leader must adapt the leadership style to meet the needs of the followers. While every leader has to consider both relationships and effectiveness, efficiency is determined by a leader's ability to analyze a situation, evaluate the readiness of followers, and make appropriate decisions. Several tools being used to assist leaders in understanding this behavior are the DISC Test, [5] LEAD Inventory, [6] and *How to Be a More Effective Church Leader*.[7]

3. Greater Pastoral Authority

The trend in growing churches is for the pastoral staff, especially the senior pastor, to take on a much more authoritative role in leading the church, generating the vision, and mobilizing the congregation. This is demonstrated in the following diagram:

Greater Pastoral Authority

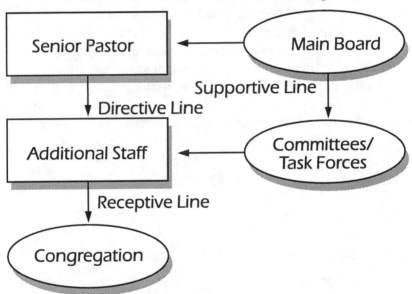

The senior pastor and staff represent the decisive line of leadership. They are aware of what is happening in the church and have the responsibility and authority to lead. The main boards and committees represent the supportive line of the leadership. They provide insight and encouragement to the staff. The role of these supportive groups is to set policies within which the staff exercise leadership authority. The congregation represents the receptive line. Most people are not aware of what takes place during a given week in a church, so they delegate authority to selected leaders.

4. Pastoral Care Through Small Groups

"Preventative" and "reactive" are two types of pastoral care offered by most churches. With reactive pastoral care, church leadership responds to each individual's call for help. Using this system of care, leaders find themselves in a "fire-fighting" mode much of the time. The second type of pastoral care is preventative in nature. Problems are anticipated and planned for in advance so that when they arise, a way already exists to offer personal care.

Most churches find themselves in the reactive style. When the leadership does not respond quickly to an issue, there are hurt feelings and a sense of failed leadership. Today's effective churches reach their full potential by giving pastoral care ministries to the congregation at large, and specifically, to small group leaders. Where else will the average person find support in times of trial and/or temptation? Where else will a member be able to gain the encouragement of other people with like ideas and needs? Where else can people know that a group of people will be praying for them and with them throughout a time of struggle?

Small groups offer the ideal site for pastoral care. Small-group leadership is ready and equipped by the growing church. This list of possible areas are often covered in the training of small-group leaders:

▲ Listening Skills

▲ Basic Counseling Techniques

▲ Hospital Visitation

▲ Discipleship

▲ Follow-up of New Believers

▲ Biblical Hermenuetics

▲ People Skills (ability to work with others)

▲ Time Management

▲ Administration (planning and follow-through)

▲ Prayer

▲ Servant Leadership

5. Telecare Ministry

People are busy. They are more interested in a call on the phone than a call to the home. If we visit people at home, they must straighten up the house and do the dishes. This is an inconvenience for two out of three households where both people work outside the home and have little time to clean up, except on the weekends.

Despite this fact, many desire to see the church as a place to make and cultivate friendships. George Barna in a 1992-93 study identified the main places where friendships are made both for the Christian and the non-Christian. His study found church as a predominant place to both groups.[8]

Non-Christians			
Work **45%**	Church **32%**	Clubs **22%**	School **20%**

Christians			
Church **75%**	Work **45%**	Clubs **18%**	Community Groups **18%**

People come to church looking for support. The telecare ministry provides a way of getting into a home without the threat or perceived expectations of a visit (see chap. 8).

6. Experimental Philosophy

Breakthroughs occur when someone creatively ignores the rules. For example, for years it was assumed that Sunday morning was the time for preaching to believers. Sunday evening, the Sunday School, or special evangelistic events were used for reaching the unchurched.

However, in the late 1970s the idea surfaced that maybe by ignoring the standing rule that Sunday morning was for believers, and targeting the Sunday worship service to the unchurched, many people might be brought into the church. And so, the seeker service was started. Today's leaders risk breaking the rules so that they may increase their effectiveness in ministry.

7. Result-oriented Leadership

Rarely did we used to hear of a pastor being fired. Congregations viewed their pastor as God's anointed and, unless there was a clear case of unethical behavior, the pastor stayed until God called him to another ministry.

Right or wrong, this is no longer the case. Our fast-paced, action-oriented society now expects that leaders produce results. Pastors and other church leaders find pink slips coming their way. Most often the charge is incompetence or a vague, "You're just not the leader for us."

Researcher George Barna surveyed 1,044 pastors and surprisingly these were his findings:

▲ Four percent of all pastors could not communicate a clear vision for their church.

▲ Only 6 percent of all pastors claim to have the spiritual gift of leadership.[9]

The inference from Barna's research is that most senior pastors are trained to communicate rather than lead. While public and private communication skills are necessary, they do not necessarily transfer over to leadership. Today's church needs leaders!

Leading in Changing Times

Some people claim that leaders are born and that signs of leadership assert themselves early in life. In some cases this may be true. But how many people have we known who were voted "most likely to succeed" but never made their mark on the world?

We believe leadership is an acquired trait, a trait forged in the battles—successes and failures—of life. Courage is the kernel of leadership.

1. Take Time to Dream

At age fifty, William Pinkney realized that if he had any dreams he wanted to fulfill, he'd better get to fulfilling them. His dream was to make a solo voyage around the world by sailboat. In order to fulfill his dream he had to raise over $400,000 to outfit his boat with computer equipment and a shortwave radio. On August 5, 1990, Pinkney left Boston harbor in his forty-seven-foot sailboat, the *Commitment,* and headed for the world. Two years later, on June 9, 1992, he once again docked in Boston harbor.

As a leader he learned that the hardest thing to bear was the solitude. He once went for sixty-five days without seeing another soul. "When there are high waves and strong winds, you've got to act, and you're focused on that. But when it's quiet, boredom is difficult to fight," writes Pinkney.[10]

A leader with a vision will always beat one with an agenda.

Vision is two-pronged. It consists of a "Guiding Philosophy," a set of core values, and a "Bold Mission," made up of a BHAG: Big, Hairy, Audacious Goal.[11]

Developing a vision takes at least five steps.

Step 1: Define what God wants. Begin by making a long written list of what you sense God wants your church to do. Look at your church as part of a larger picture. How does it fit in to the social structure of your community? Your city? Your county? Your state? Your nation? Your world? How will any of these areas be any different because your church is there? What is your vision to touch the hearts, minds, and souls of the people in your community?

After making your list, sift through it several times, striking out the weaker ideas each time. As your list grows smaller, you will find that the value remaining has grown greater. Visit other churches to see what they are doing. Tom Peters, best-selling author and business consultant, notes a bureaucratic (and doomed) organization will reject ideas that are "Not Invented Here." Companies and nations on the rise prefer the motto: "Swiped with Pride from the Best."[12]

Step 2: Keep the dream alive. Make a habit of thinking about your dream. Write your dream in graphic detail, visualizing what you see happening. Write it purposefully: Why is your vision important? Precisely: What do you see taking place? Pictorially: What will the end product look like?

The biggest mistake church leaders make is to communicate the vision one time and then think that everyone has got it. As a rule of thumb, plan on communicating your vision a minimum of five different ways every year until the vision is reached. Consider using some of the following ideas:

▲ Plan a "state of the church day" worship service in January of every year to communicate your vision.

▲ Interview people who illustrate the vision from the pulpit.

▲ Tell stories of other churches, people, and organizations that have accomplished a great vision.

▲ Make banners to hang in the church auditorium, the fellowship hall, or other rooms in the church building to communicate your vision.

▲ Write articles in your church newsletter or program (bulletin) about your vision.

▲ Personally visit every member of your church to share your vision and answer questions about it.

▲ Take church leaders to seminars and workshops which will help them catch the spirit of the vision.

▲ Host a yearly leadership retreat for brainstorming on how to reach your vision.

▲ Update the congregation on the progress toward the vision at least quarterly.

▲ Mention your vision and how your church's ministry contributes to its accomplishment at least monthly from the pulpit.

Step 3: Believe your vision will happen. Our Lord encourages us to "Walk in wisdom toward those who are outside, redeeming the time" (Col. 4:5, NKJV). "Time" is a limited season when people are open to the good news of Jesus Christ. Our job is to quickly take advantage of the opportunities that are ours to win people to Christ since the season (time) is changing and opportunities that are here now will soon be gone.

Read your vision every day. Begin the first step to get where you want to be. Take a class, make a phone call—as the Nike slogan says, "Just Do It!"

Step 4: Be grateful. Make a list of your current blessings and read it everyday. One of our favorite passages of Scripture describing this process for overcoming frustration and anxiety is Philippians 4:4–9 which ends with a list of good things to think about. "Finally, brothers, whatever is true, whatever is noble, whatever is right, whatever is pure, whatever is lovely, whatever is admirable, if anything is excellent or praiseworthy—think about such things" (v. 8).

Express your gratitude for each of the items on your list. As the Scripture commands, "Be joyful always; pray continually; give thanks in all circumstances; for this is God's will for you in Christ Jesus" (1 Thess. 5:16–18).

Step 5: Be patient. Less can be accomplished in one year than you think but more can be accomplished in five years than you think. As a rule of thumb, if your church is located in the context of a city, it will take a minimum of five years to develop, communicate, and accomplish your vision. If your church is located in a more rural context, it may take as many as ten to twelve years to see it happen. But it can happen as you plant, water, and allow God to give the increase (1 Cor. 3:6).

2. Develop a Strategic Plan

The environment in which leaders find themselves today demands that they take time away from regular responsibilities to plan. Strategic planning is essential to leadership and is often overlooked. Many times, leadership functions in a survival mode. "Oh, boy . . . here comes Easter. What are we going to do? . . . We made it through Easter but here comes Vacation Bible School. What should we plan for in September? Christmas? Got any ideas?" It can be a vicious cycle unless addressed with strategic planning. Here are some general ideas to get you started.

First, strategic planning is God's will. Many leaders hesitate to do too much planning, fearing that they are demonstrating a lack of faith. Nothing could be farther from the truth. The Holy Spirit knows the future as well as the moment. Planning, by its very nature, increases faith by encouraging leaders to look at the future, anticipating the results by setting goals and trusting God to bring about the results. Proverbs says it best, "Commit your works to the Lord, and your plans will be established" (Prov. 16:3, NASB; see also 16:1–2, 9–11).

Second, involve the core leaders with the input of the people at large. The key is communication. The people want to know what is going to happen. They want to have a say in the change process, so take surveys and talk with small groups to access their ideas.

Third, planning overcomes institutional inertia. Any organization can become complacent and need a push to get it moving again. Organizational structure delays movement and change by its very nature. Planning provides a mechanism that redirects the movement of an organization and overcomes the "We've never done it that way before" attitudes.

Lastly, strategic planning creates a climate for growth. Any successful organization plans long range. It evaluates the present, anticipates the future, and plans accordingly. When strategic planning is motivated by the leadership, the resultant desire to plan for the following years will be based upon today's successes and failures.

3. Learn to Be a Change Agent

The key difference between leaders and managers is that leaders create change. No one really likes change, but growth demands it. Even in the physical realm, for a child to grow into adolescence and past puberty, change occurs in the body. This can also be said of the church as a body. Dr. Carl George, director of the Charles E. Fuller Institute of Evangelism and Church Growth, recently presented a new paradigm which he has named, "The Meta-Church."

He explains, "I believe churches grow best if they find a model that God is blessing. Apparently, then, God is working through a number of different models, from traditional to contemporary, and the many nuances in between."[13] The key word in this quote is the word "find." Leaders identify those areas of responsiveness and receptivity in the community and focus their energies and resources in those directions.

Recognizing that change is both necessary and painful, here are seven guidelines to remember when initiating change in any organization.

Guideline #1: Have a good reason for the change. Cultural changes are usually not well accepted and thus result in resistance. Take change seriously. Make sure you understand why you are making the change and that it is a necessary part of the strategic planning of the leadership.

Guideline #2: Involve people in the process of change. People who are involved in creating change are less likely to resist the changes. Being a part of the planning process gives people a sense of control. We recommend creating a transition leadership team (not a committee) to initiate the process of change.

This team should include a cross-section of your group and have as their function to plan, anticipate, troubleshoot, coordinate, and focus the change efforts. "Great leaders don't tell people how to do the job," General H. Norman Schwarzkopf said in *Management Review*. Instead, they communicate what needs to be done and establish standards. "People want to know what is expected of them," he continued. The best leaders strive to create an environment in which people can achieve their own success.[14]

Guideline #3: Appoint a person to be in charge of the process. Every change needs a leader. Select someone who is seen in a positive light by the group being affected. He or she does not have to be a member of the governing leadership, but this must be someone who understands the vision and the direction of the leadership.

Guideline #4: Provide training in new values and behavior. People need education and guidance in understanding what the "new way" consists of and why it is more desirable. Training brings groups together. It allows them to express their concerns and reinforce newly learned skills. Try hosting an occasional three-hour seminar for leaders and concerned supporters as a means of educating them to the need for change.

Guideline #5: Use outside help for education and motivation. Outside resource people have up to ten times the authority over someone from the inside. Use this powerful tool by bringing in a church consultant who can reinforce the direction you want to go.

Guideline #6: Establish visible symbols of change. Encourage the development of newsletters, logos or slogans, and events to help celebrate and reflect the change. Many churches are turning to media as a primary means of updating the change process. For instance, one church began the 1993 year with a call to the church to reach "93 in 93." Their goal was to win to Christ ninety-three unchurched families during the year.

A video documentary was filmed telling the story of three different individuals who had found Christ in their church. It was shown on a Sunday morning to illustrate the vision for the coming year. Bookmarks were passed out in January and a time of personal reflection and commitment was provided in the service for the worshipers to identify who they could begin praying for in 1993 to come to Jesus. Three months into the year, this church had seen forty-two families touched by the gospel and now attending their church. So that the vision of "93 in 93" would not get stale, a media presentation highlighting one of the families touched by their ministry was shown during the services . . . a symbol of change.

Guideline #7: Acknowledge and reward the people involved. As change takes place, and people are accepting the results and process, take time to recognize and recall the achievements of the people who made it happen. Acknowledge the struggle and sacrifices people made and how their contribution has not been overlooked. Allow them to see that this has been a team effort. We recommend personal interviews from the pulpit or special recognition services. If appropriate in your church, encourage applause for those who have contributed to the change efforts.

Most of the revolutionary improvements in churches occur by gradual, incremental improvements, based on suggestions from workers, volunteers, and leaders. These "baby steps" are consistent, easy to implement, and less disruptive than major, global changes that emanate from above.

A new concept in the United States, which was borrowed from the Japanese, is *kaizen*. It means "continuous improvement" and builds into the individual the idea that every worker is responsible to do more than maintain the status quo; part of the job is to suggest small improvements, which could improve efficiency or quality. Build a *kaizen* attitude among your people so that they do not just tolerate change but become a part of the process of creating change.

4. Make Prayer a Priority

The events of our lives are mirror images of our thoughts. The best expression of our thoughts is our prayer life. What do we pray about? What do we find ourselves repeating in our prayers? Like most of us, you likely find yourself repeating certain ideas or themes in your prayer life. What themes do you hear yourself praying? These themes reflect your major thoughts, and you will tend to move in the direction of your major thoughts.

Two strategic things happen when we pray. One, we draw closer to God as we get to know and trust Him more. Two, we engage in a battle—spiritual warfare. In doing so we are recapturing from the enemy that which he has no right to, and we are helping to build the kingdom of God in our church and the lives of all those for whom we pray. Have you ever wondered why Satan puts up such a fight—resists so hard our attempts to pray? Does not this in itself tell us something vital about prayer? Would Satan waste his time on something that does not matter? No, he's too smart for that.

To give you just a taste of what could happen, think about your last difficult board meeting or congregational meeting. What would have been different if more strategic prayer had been added?

What if a specific team of intercessors as well as other concerned members and leaders had focused positive prayer on the meeting for days and weeks preceding it? What if there had been a group of intercessors in the audience or a nearby room praying the whole time for the meeting? What if the leaders had specifically prayed for unity and for the will of God to be done? What if they had prayed that each individual would be willing to lay aside his own interests in order to have the best interests of the whole met?

What would have happened if we were committed to stopping when things started to get difficult or tense and *prayed*, asking the Lord to give fresh insight and control to all and show His thoughts on the matter? How would this have affected the tone and emotional level of the meeting, the hearts of those participating, the relationships (or lack of them) of those who were not originally in agreement? What about the future working relationships of the members? These same questions can be applied to any church decision-making body.

Paul said in Ephesians 4:13, "Till we all come in to unity of the faith" (NKJV). Prayer was a key part of doing this in the first century. It is just as vital in reaching such unity in changing times. Prayer does change things.

5. Communicate Your Vision

Pericles, ruler of ancient Greece, had a realistic view of his own gifts: "When Pericles speaks, they say, 'How well he speaks.' When Demosthenes speaks, they say, 'Let us march.'" Leadership and success lie beyond facts. They lie with the ability to persuade.

If you have ever watched a marathon you likely have noticed the phenomenon of staggering. At the beginning all of the racers are together at the starting line. But even though someone is out front setting an average pace, gaps will open up between runners. Someone experiences a strain in a calf muscle and slows down a bit. Another runner peaks out before the race and doesn't have the energy to stay up. Gradually more and more space is seen between runners.

As the race wears on, the gaps between runners gets greater and greater. At this point, even though all runners may be competing at the same pace, it is difficult for those farther back to ever catch up. To do so means expending greater energy than those in front. The front runner is setting the pace, but every time another runner slows down it lengthens the line of runners.

Each person's speed depends, to some degree, on the speed of the one in front of him. This is particularly true when the lead runner is out of sight. Psychologically, a runner looks at the person in front who can be seen. The pace is determined by the runners immediately in front of their positions. The lead runner may be going faster or slower, but if the runners in back cannot see the lead runner, who's to know?

Catching the vision is delayed by the distance between the front runner (pastor or other visionary) and those farther back who have yet to catch and own the vision. In reality, reaching the vision only happens when *everyone* completes the race. If the pastor is too far out in front, the gaps widen, the pace slows, and accomplishing the vision takes longer.

In order for a church to grow we optimize the entire system, not just one or two areas. To grow, everyone must cross the finish line. Everyone must complete his or her task. While the lead runner may finish (complete one area of ministry), optimum growth potential is not reached until all finish the race.

Thus, the longer it takes to communicate the vision, the longer it will take to reach optimum performance. The pastor or other visionary leaders must set the pace but stay in sight of those who have not caught the vision yet. To get out of sight means a slowing of results.

Horace Greeley used to say that the best way to write an editorial was to write it to the best of your ability, then cut it in the middle and print the last half.

The same applies to speaking. Shoot arrows, not logs!

6. Start a Continuing Education Program

In the state of Oregon one can see the deep ruts left by wagon trains traveling along the Oregon Trail. Year after year the constant movement of wagon wheels over the same terrain caused deep gouges to develop in the ground. As more wagons traveled the same route, the ruts got deeper until the actual evidence of wagon wheels was left for later generations to observe in the hard rock.

Occasionally, wagons would get into one of these ruts and, to their surprise, realize that they couldn't get out. They had to travel the entire length of the rut whether they wished to or not.

Leaders who have been in the same ministry for awhile find the tendency is to settle into ruts, doing things the same way. But, as we have noted throughout, times have changed, and while a particular way of doing ministry may have worked in the past, today it may be purely a rut.

To get out of the ruts of ministry, develop a creative spirit by attending some continuing education program. Attend workshops, seminars, or invest in formal schooling such as a doctor of ministry program. And, perhaps most importantly, keep up with your reading. An interesting insight into doctor of ministry programs relates to the required reading. Such formal programs call for the students to read fifteen to twenty-five books for each course or about three thousand pages of reading. Surveys of graduates reveals that the required reading is one of the highlights of the program. The reason? Most pastors just do not schedule the time for keeping up with their reading after they leave seminary or other formal schooling. Unfortunately, as with many careers, changes are happening so quickly that what pastors learn in a seminar is out of date within five to ten years.

Here are some ideas for carving out the time for reading.

Idea #1: Realize it is impossible to read everything. Even if we were able to read every journal, book, and periodical available, we still would not know it all. In fact, we would not know as much about our world as Galileo or Aristotle knew about theirs. So relax! Try ideas #2–#7.

Idea #2: Determine what is germane to your work. Instead of trying to read everything that you think you should, determine what is essential to your life and interests. List the books, magazines, and journals that are directly related to your field. Narrow your list down to the germane.

Idea #3: Use vicarious readers. Ask two or three people to read for you. You read what is germane (see idea #2) and ask your vicarious readers to read the rest, passing along only copies of quotations or articles that might be significant to your ministry.

Idea #4: Select reading based on reading lists. Ask respected leaders in your field of interest to provide reading lists of the top ten books or articles they would recommend. Then limit your initial reading to items found on their lists. As a start, select one of the lists we have suggested at the end of each chapter in this book.

Idea #5: Use the shard method. Purchase any magazines, newspapers, or journals you think look interesting. Let them stack up on a shelf until they reach the shelf above. Then take the time to skim through them tearing out the articles that strike you as important to your life and ministry. Throw the rest away. You will then have the shards that will be meaningful reading.

Idea #6: Scan; don't read. Avoid the feeling that you must read everything word-for-word. Develop the habit of scanning or skimming the headlines. Stop only to read thoroughly those articles that seem key to your ministry.

Idea #7: Practice the ambush technique. Listen to what your colleagues say are the best books, articles, newsletters, and journals to read. After you've heard the same one recommended repeatedly, then ambush it by reading only that one book, article, newsletter, or journal.

An old adage says leaders are readers. A corollary to that is leaders are learners. Improve yourself! A church can not rise above the quality of its leadership. As people see you getting better, they follow suit. How much have they seen you improve lately?

7. Control Your Time

One of the new discoveries in modern sports psychology is that performance comes in waves. We cannot be at our best all the time, so we have to pick our times.

Athletes call this process "periodization." Through exercise, sleep, and eating habits, they try to pick the peak times for their performance. When it works, they often perform far beyond normal ability. It is commonly said they are in a "zone." Zoning occurs when mental, physical, and emotional balance peak at once. Sports psychologists call this Ideal Performance State (IPS).

Pastors have observed this phenomenon for years. Beginning about Tuesday, pastors begin to pray, plan, study, and prepare to speak on Sunday. Monday, typically, becomes a day to let down. This "periodization" often leads to a positive feeling on Sunday and a depressed feeling on Monday.

What is your wave? When do you tend to peak, and when do you tend to recover? How long does it take you to recover? Some methods for controlling your wave are to keep regular sleep patterns, exercise on a regular time schedule, set goals, and maintain a positive mind set.

Almost any leader can control his personal IPS and learn to peak at key times. But we have to take control in two key areas: control of our own life in eating, exercise, and thinking habits; control of our time for meetings, confrontations, counseling, speaking, and study.

8. Set Some Personal Goals

As a young man, Benjamin Franklin resolved to attain the habits of virtue that would lead to success by making a game out of self-improvement. He wrote thirteen key virtues in a notebook, one to a page, and checked off each instance in the day when he failed in one of them. He focused on one virtue per week, running through his list four times, every year, until he had developed the habit of it. His thirteen virtues and goals were:

1. Temperance
2. Silence
3. Order
4. Resolution
5. Frugality
6. Industry
7. Sincerity
8. Justice
9. Moderation
10. Cleanliness
11. Tranquillity
12. Chastity
13. Humility[15]

This is strikingly similar to Paul's list we mentioned above, given in Philippians 4:8. Leaders set personal goals and work toward them on a regular basis.

9. Build on Your Strengths

We've all heard of athletes who have faced criticism and come back to prove their detractors wrong. Larry Rosenthal was one such player. He grew up on the sand lots in baseball's early years and eventually made it all the way to the mighty New York Yankees, playing eight years for them in the outfield. However, in the battle for the 1944 pennant race, the Yankees traded him to the lowly Philadelphia Athletics. But, as any good story would have it, he had the last laugh. It was a ninth-inning home run for the A's by Rosenthal that knocked the Yankees out of the pennant race, giving the pennant that year for the first and only time to the St. Louis Browns. Rosenthal built on his strengths and found success even with a disappointing trade.

Coauthor Glen Martin likes to say that there are three types of leaders—risk-takers, caretakers, and undertakers. How would you put these three words—mediocrity, failure, and success—in order. If you put success first, followed by failure, and then mediocrity, you're a risk-taker. The reason? Failure is closer to success than mediocrity.

Should we shore up our weaknesses or build on our strengths? In pastoring, business, or war, we will experience the greatest success by reinforcing our strengths. The *blitzkrieg*, or "lightning war," tactic used by the Germans at the start of World War II is an example of reinforcing strength. The Germans would attack across a wide front. The front line commander had a simple mission: penetrate rapidly. If he met resistance, he was to lead his men around the trouble spot until he got through. The mission of headquarters in the rear was to secure the path behind the advancing forces. A *blitzkrieg* focuses on opportunities instead of problems.

To reinforce your strengths, spend time, money, and energy supporting what works for you. Where have you experienced the most empowerment in ministry? What has provided the results? Allocate your resources of time, thought, and work to those areas. If you support only your weaknesses, your leadership will be built around defending yourself instead of attacking opportunities. You will build your leadership around short-term problem-solving (putting out fires) rather than long-term results.

Kayakers and river rafters know that whatever you do, the river keeps running. If you don't make a decision, life will make one for you. Leaders cause a splash. A weak leader only skips across the water, generating weak ripples and leaving everyone to fend for himself. Ambiguous leadership produces ambiguous results! Create the future! Be a leader!

▼

NOTES

[1] Robert Holmes, "Catch the Spirit" *Parables* (Platteville, Colo.: United Methodist Committee on Communications), 4.

[2] John Wesley, as quoted by E.M. Bounds in *Power Through Prayer* (Grand Rapids, Mich.: Zondervan, 1980), 71.

[3] William C. Cook, *Success, Motivation, and the Scriptures* (Nashville: Broadman Press, 1974), 9.

[4] Robert Blake and Jane Mouton, *The Managerial Grid III* (Houston: Gulf Publishing Co., 1985), 12.

[5] Published by Performax Systems International, Inc. (Minneapolis, Minn.: Carlson Learning Co., 1977).

[6] Available from Pfeiffer & Company, 8517 Production Avenue, San Diego, Calif., 92121; (619) 578-2042.

[7] Norman Shawchuck, *How to Be a More Effective Church Leader* (Irvine, Calif.: Spiritual Growth Resources, 1981); (800) 359-7363.

[8] Adapted from *The Barna Report* 1992-93, George Barna (Ventura, Calif.: Regal Books, 1992), 131.

[9] George Barna, *Today's Pastors* (Ventura, Calif.: Regal Books, 1993), 118-122.

[10] Esaki-Smith, Anna, "Fantastic Voyage," *Success* (February 1993), 50-51.

[11] Reported in "Inside Track," *Success* (February 1993), 24.

[12] Quoted by Anderson and Poe in "A Culture of Achievement," *Leadership* (June 1992), 34.

[13] Carl F. George, *How to Break Growth Barriers* (Grand Rapids, Mich.: Baker Book House, 1993), 67.

[14] *Success*, 24.

[15] Anderson and Poe, 34.

RESOURCES

Tapes:

Biehl, Bob. *Leadership Confidence.* Available from Masterplanning Group International, Box 6128, Laguna Niguel, CA 92607; (800) 443-1976. Also available: *Mentoring: How to Find a Mentor, and How to Become One, Masterplanning Your Church, Focusing Your Life, LifeWork, Defining Your . . .*

George, Carl and Logan, Robert. *How to Lead and Manage the Local Church: Self-Study Kit.* Available from the Charles E. Fuller Institute of Evangelism & Church Growth, P. O. Box 91990, Pasadena, CA 91109-1990; (800) 999-9578.

Lacey, Walt. *L-E-A-D Personality Inventory.* Available from the Church Growth Institute, P. O. Box 4404, Lynchburg, VA 24502; (800) 553-GROW.

Evaluation Tools:

Role Preference Inventory. Available from Masterplanning Group International, Box 6128, Laguna Niguel, CA 92607; (800) 443-1976.

Performax DISC Test. Available from The Church Growth Network, 3630 Camelia Dr., San Bernardino, CA 92404; 909-882-5386.

Spiritual Gifts Inventory and *LEAD Personality Inventory.* Available from the Church Growth Institute, P. O. Box 4404, Lynchburg, VA 24502. (800) 553-GROW.

For Further Reading:

Anderson, Leith. *Dying for Change.* Minneapolis: Bethany House Publishers, 1990.

Barna, George. *The Power of Vision.* Ventura, Calif.: Regal Books, 1992.

Barna. *Today's Pastors.* Ventura, Calif.: Regal Books, 1993.

Bennis, Warren. *On Becoming a Leader.* Reading, Mass.: Addison-Wesley Pub., 1989. (See also *Leaders* by Bennis and Nanus).

Callahan, Kennon L. *Effective Church Leadership: Building on the Twelve Keys.* New York: Harper & Row, 1990.

Dale, Robert. *To Dream Again.* Nashville: Broadman Press, 1981.

Dale, Robert. *Keeping the Dream Alive.* Nashville: Broadman Press, 1988.

George, Carl F. and Logan, Robert. *Leading & Managing Your Church.* Old Tappan,N. J.: Fleming H. Revell Co., 1987.

Malphurs, Aubrey. *Developing a Vision for Ministry in the 21st Century.* Grand Rapids, Mich.: Baker Book House, 1992.

5

If you're getting the job done,
I like the way you're doing it.
—Pastor Rick Warren

I have found in traveling in a stagecoach that it is often a comfort
to shift one's position and be bruised in a new place.
—Washington Irving

ADMINISTRATION

Read the following story of two churches and then guess which church is the growing church.

Church #1: In May a proposal was brought to the board to begin a preschool as an outreach ministry to young couples and single parents near the church. The idea found acceptance with church leaders who immediately began to investigate the possibilities. In June a decision was made to proceed. The challenge was presented to the congregation, and twelve thousand dollars was raised through gifts and donations. Remodeling took place over the summer to prepare the church faculties to house the preschool. A preschool director was hired, supplies purchased, and advertising started. The preschool opened the first week of September with twelve students.

Church #2: In May a proposal was brought to the board to begin a preschool as an outreach ministry to young couples and single parents near the church. The idea found some acceptance with the church leaders who decided to enter into a full investigation of the possibilities. A research committee was appointed and took fifteen months to study the issues surrounding the project. After nearly a year and a half of study, the board voted not to move ahead with the project.

If you guessed church #1 is the growing one, you are correct. Today it boasts nearly one hundred preschoolers. In the ten years since it opened, over fifty families have been introduced to Christ and the church, and about 50 percent of all who join testify that their first exposure to the church was through the preschool.

And the second church? In the same ten-year period it has lost close to half of its worshipers. The leaders have the reputation of being indecisive procrastinators. Future leaders become frustrated and eventually move on to other places of worship. Today there is a downward spiral which is dragging the morale and vitality along with it.

Administration Trends

We live in a new era of administration. No longer can churches afford to just maintain. People expect results; and if they do not see movement in the overall direction of the church's goals, they will move on to a ministry that appears to be accomplishing its goals.

Administration

That was then...	This is now...
▲ Committee	▲ Task force
▲ Pastor doing administration	▲ Pastor of administration
▲ Simple organization	▲ Complex organization
▲ Program driven	▲ Purpose driven
▲ Manual record keeping	▲ Computerized records
▲ Volunteer secretaries	▲ Professional secretaries
▲ Volunteer support staff	▲ Professional support staff
▲ Rigid rules	▲ Flexible guidelines
▲ Low-tech	▲ High-tech
▲ Disruptive changes	▲ Controlled changes
▲ Hide information	▲ Share information
▲ Focus on past	▲ Focus on future
▲ Longer decision making	▲ Faster decision making
▲ Flying solo	▲ Flying in formation

1. Simple Structure

Alvin Toffler says, "Each age produces a form of organization appropriate to its own tempo."[1] Today, churches grow as they develop an organizational structure which allows them to take advantage of ministry opportunities. They create temporary task forces, rather than long-term committees. Their motto: if you can do it with one person, why use a committee? Committees produce complexity instead of leadership. Committees don't lead; groups don't lead; only people lead. Search the parks in any city; you will see dozens of statues of leaders—and not one of a committee!

2. Flying in Formation

There is a sacred rule in the Air Force: Always keep formation. The only way to survive in air-to-air combat is to stay together and protect each other. While there are times, of course, when it is "every man for himself," the general rule holds true in any team situation. No matter how much people do or how engaging their personalities are, they will not accomplish much if they cannot work through others.

We can get a lot done if we are not concerned about who gets the credit for it. As someone once said, "Keep your eyes on the prize and out of the mirror." In conventional jobs, you get paid for what you do alone. In the church, you are rewarded for mentoring people and building up their skills. Tommy Lasorda, manager of the Los Angeles Dodgers, tells his players, "Playing for yourself wins trophies; playing for your team wins championships."

3. Purpose Driven

On a warm August morning more than five centuries ago, Christopher Columbus embarked from a small seaport near Palos, Spain. As the joke goes, when he left, he didn't know where he was going. When he got there, he didn't know where he was. And when he returned, he didn't know where he had been. What he did know, of course, was his purpose. And it was commitment and belief in his purpose which kept him going. When his crew lost faith and the long voyage seemed futile, he kept going. Even though he didn't accomplish his exact purpose, it was his pursuit of it that led him to discover something even greater—the new world.

The attitude at the top of any organization ripples through everything that happens. An ambiguous purpose produces mediocre results. A clearly defined purpose provides a solid foundation for growth. Today's growing churches are purpose driven.

4. Administrative Pastors

The traditional paradigm of the senior pastor is that of a jack-of-all-trades role. Older senior pastors remember preaching three times a week, visiting every afternoon, organizing the church office, coordinating all church functions, and, in some cases, even paying the bills. In less complex times that was a functional role. Today such a method does not seem to work as well. We cannot do today's ministry with yesterday's methods and be effective tomorrow.

The complexity of our information age has created specialized role opportunities often quite divergent from the traditional role. One of these new opportunities is the pastor of administration. People filling this position take responsibility for such things as payroll, office management, accounting, facility coordination.

5. Computerized Records

Dr. Win Arn, founder and director of the influential Institute for American Church Growth, was a man ahead of his time. As an example of his foresight, in the early 1980s he saw the ministry potential of computers being used by churches. True to his vision, he started a new company to provide this new resource to local churches. He secured a professional firm to develop software which was sensitive to church growth concepts, and he hired a former IBM executive to run the fledgling company. He secured appropriate hardware and began marketing his products to churches. Unfortunately, churches were not quite ready for computers in the early 1980s, and the company was eventually sold.

His vision, however, was correct. Today it is becoming unusual not to find a computer in the church office. Computer tools free us from administrivia so we can focus on our main job—seeking and saving the lost. Edward R. McCracken, president and CEO of Silicon Graphics, stated: "Technology is a business tool, not a panacea for enterprise. It's what we do with technology that counts."[2]

6. Professional Secretaries

Church secretaries are a mainstay in the church office. Many church secretaries actually serve the function of administrative pastor, although most churches would not be willing to give them that title.

While church secretaries are not new to the church, what is new is the move from using volunteers to that of hiring professionals. In place of the volunteer working in the office a few days a week, churches now seek out secretaries who are computer literate and can take dictation. Today's secretary has excellent people skills and is able to organize and oversee others in a professional office environment.

7. Clear Job Descriptions

Early in this century, as the story goes, an ad appeared in the *Times* of London. It read: "Men wanted for hazardous journey. Low wages, bitter cold, long hours of complete darkness. Safe return doubtful. Honor and recognition in the event of success." The ad was signed by E. Shackleton. Ernest Shackleton was looking for a crew to take on his quest to discover the South Pole. The next morning, over five thousand men were waiting outside the *Times'* offices, and thus Shackleton reached the pole in 1907. People respond to the challenge of greatness![3]

The appeal of this advertisement was its challenge. However, what made it work was its clear description of what was required. Growing churches in our changing world find that clear ministry descriptions are an effective way to recruit people for ministry roles. People are not as apt to volunteer for an open-ended position where they are uncertain of what is required. Today's recruitment strategies used by growing churches include careful use of detailed job descriptions.

Improving Administration in Changing Times

An advertisement for the Dial Corporation, makers of products such as Breck shampoo and Dial soap, begins with the statement: "Either you shape the future, or the future shapes you." The ad continues: "Change or be changed. Act or be acted upon."[4]

These are good words for us to ponder as we consider the following ideas for improving the administrative aspects of our churches.

1. Define Your Core Values

Core values are the basic concepts a church holds in high regard. Some churches see tradition as a core value. Others place high value on being a family church where everyone knows everyone else. Still others value flexibility and the ability to change programs at will.

Unfortunately, many core values are tacit or unspoken values. Changes in values take place at an extremely slow pace, and being unaware of these tacit rules provides many traps for the new pastor or new member in a church. Core values are powerful controlling factors behind all decisions, and it is crucial that they be identified to enhance ministry.

An excellent tool for identifying core values is to develop an acrostic using your church's name. Take your church name and then use each letter as the first letter of a word describing a statement of your values. For instance, here is the values statement of Hope Bible Church, which is actually a composite of several real churches.

High concern for people
Obedience to God
Personal spiritual growth
Encouragement
Becoming like Christ
Involving people
Being a disciple-making church
Love of the Word of God
Emphasis on families

A quick reading of this acrostic gives one a fairly clear idea of what this church values.

2. Write a New Purpose Statement

No businesses in history have grown as fast as direct selling organizations (DSOs). Companies such as Amway, Nu Skin, and Mary Kay Cosmetics are popular examples. Unlike older, bureaucratically driven companies, a DSO is purpose driven. People join a DSO in part out of a common bonding to the purpose of the founder.

No organization has a greater purpose than the church. However, if you take a survey of worshipers in the average church, you will find that few of them can articulate the church's purpose statement. While most churches already have a purpose statement, often it is confusing as written into the church constitution or so out-of-date that it doesn't communicate to today's audience.

A purpose statement is the biblical reason a church exists. It has at least three key aspects.

▲ It is biblical: A purpose statement should have its foundation clearly in God's Word.

▲ It is perpetual: Although a purpose statement may at times be restated to communicate to a new generation of people, it essentially is unchanging.

▲ It is understandable: A purpose statement must be communicated clearly so that people easily remember it and understand what it means.

Write a new purpose statement, keeping it under twenty-five words in length.

3. Minimize Differences; Maximize Potential

In the 1800s fire fighting in Los Angeles was accomplished through bucket brigades. This was a slow process and not a very good way to win the battle against fire.

On November 20, 1869, Engine Company Number One was formed as the first step in developing a complete fire department. In 1874 and 1875, two new engine companies were formed: the Thirty-Eights Engine Company (named in honor of the original 38 volunteers) and the Confidence Engine Company.

Over the years, these two engine companies became fierce rivals. When a fire alarm sounded, both engine companies would race to see who would reach the fire first. People would turn out to see the fire and take bets on which engine company would get there first. The talk of the town the next day focused on who got there first. The dark side of this happy rivalry is that getting to the fire became the main thing. The fire itself was secondary.[5]

Historically, factions within churches have acted in the same manner. Called to "seek and save the lost," church members have in many cases fought over petty issues while forgetting their God-given purpose. The pluralism and complexity of our information age is ripe for further division. Church leaders correctly are empowered to protect the flock of God against unbiblical teaching (Acts 20:28–31), but we must also maintain the unity of the body.

Effective churches in our changing times find it beneficial to minimize the differences among people and to maximize the potential. For example, at one time it was common for churches to spend great amounts of time debating such issues as dancing, going to movies, and watching television. Looking back, most churches now view those arguments as non-productive.

The maximizing of the differences actually minimized the ministry potential of those churches. The anger and bitterness among brothers and sisters, as well as the reputation the church gained in the unchurched community, actually worked against a church's purpose to "seek and save the lost." Churches became like fire engine companies, racing to win the argument, but forgetting their purpose and letting the house burn down.

Today, churches find it more productive to exercise flexibility within their doctrinal and philosophical positions. For instance, some churches which formerly fought over the issue of spiritual gifts, now find it more productive to allow their church members to make their own decisions on the subject. While the church maintains a clear teaching position on the subject and requires certain guidelines for public ministry, at the same time the church allows small groups of people within the same church to exercise spiritual gifts as they desire. The result is a minimizing of differences and a maximizing of potential.

Each local congregation needs to determine in what areas and to what degree flexibility can be exercised. But effective churches in our changing times are as flexible as possible.

4. Use a "YES" Permission System

In administrating a church, some leaders (boards) use a "NO" permission system and others use a "YES" permission system.

A "NO" permission system operates by telling people no anytime they want to do something, particularly if it is something new. This efficient system keeps people under control and protects the leaders from controversy. If the church does not grow, it is never the board's fault since the people will not get involved and use their gifts. However, if a person wants to begin a new ministry, such as a small group ministry in their home, permission to do so is withheld. Of course, they are rarely told no; they simply are told they need more training, or that the leaders are planning a small group ministry in the next year or two. However, no training is ever offered and the promised small group ministry never materializes. It is a "NO" permission system.

A "YES" permission system operates by telling people yes as much as possible. In fact, unless the request for permission directly conflicts with the church's purpose or doctrine, the answer is always yes. This system is not as efficient as the "NO" system since people are encouraged to experiment with new ministries, and experiments, of course, create a mess. But, this "YES" system tells people the leadership believes in them, and more people get involved since they know they can fail with pride.

Churches which desire to minister effectively in our changing times use a "YES" permission system. As long as a new project or ministry fits within the following seven guidelines, the answer will always be yes.

Any project should be met with a yes if it is:

▲ Doctrinally sound.

▲ Biblically based.

▲ Completely legal.

▲ Thoroughly moral.

▲ Fully ethical.

▲ Appropriate to your purpose, values, vision, and philosophy of ministry.

▲ Led by competent people who will keep the leadership informed on the progress of the project.

While there are certainly other issues to be considered, such as funding, space usage, etc., any church that greets its members with a "YES" permission system will establish a positive environment for effective ministry in our changing times.

5. Create an Experimental Atmosphere

One of the main challenges to effective ministry in changing times is how to keep a creative spirit alive. The longer a church exists, the more it falls into the trap of doing things the same way they have always been done. Growing churches keep their eyes open and encourage those who boldly try new ministries.

Stay clear of negative comments in meetings. To get past negative statements do the following: Let everyone in your meeting know that you're there to discuss new ideas, and then hand each one an M&M. Tell them "you're allowed one negative comment during the meeting. Then you must eat your M&M. Once your

M&M is gone, you can't say anything negative." Meet any further negative comments with a joking, "Be quiet and eat your M&M."[6]

6. Write Ministry Descriptions

To clarify the responsibilities of positions in your church, develop written ministry descriptions for each role.

Begin by asking each person who already serves in a role or task to write his or her own ministry description. As a guideline, ask them to outline their description around these questions.

▲ Exactly what tasks do you do?

▲ How much time in hours and minutes does each task take?

▲ Whom do you report to (or should you report to)?

▲ What qualifications, training, or experience does your task require?

▲ What could the church do to improve this ministry?

Sit down privately with each leader or volunteer and draft a workable ministry description together, using the above questions as a guideline. Work through each ministry with each person involved one-by-one; it will take some time, but you will end up with usable ministry descriptions.

7. Communicate Your Values

More and more churches are decentralizing their structure to breathe new life into the church. To keep decentralization from turning into disintegration, help everyone stay focused on the goals. Develop internal communication systems, such as newsletters, to keep people up-to-date.

Visualize your church not as an organization, but as a tribe, knitted together by common values. Every tribe has its stories which teach newcomers what it means to belong. The morals of these stories are always clear. They end (like many of Jesus' parables) with either an injunction, "Go you therefore and do likewise," or a warning, "And he was bound and thrown into the outer darkness, where there is weeping and gnashing of teeth."

Make a list of the core values your tribe holds dear—quality, service, innovation, etc. Think of an occasion when one of your members or ministries strikingly lived up to (or violated) one of those values. Write it up as a story, with a moral. Do that for each of your church's values. Use these guidelines:

▲ Always begin with a heroic deed that you witnessed or that your staff told you about.

▲ Verify all facts. The story must be true.

▲ Think of a clever title.

▲ Stick to one idea or theme.

▲ Keep the story short, no longer than one single-spaced page.

▲ Make sure the story is distributed to everyone.

▲ Frame the original and give it to the people mentioned in the story as a form of recognition.

▲ Tell the story over and over. Use it in your new members' class to communicate the values of your church.

Remember: people follow people with a vision.

Since the fall of the Berlin Wall in 1989, the world has witnessed a steady stream of historic changes, nearly all of them welcome. However, for many these changes are only appreciated as they occur outside of their sphere of involvement. It is easier to appreciate change if it is unconnected to life-as-usual in their sphere of reference.

Peter Ueberroth said, "Even as we watch much of the world transform itself, we assume America does not have to change in any fundamental way."[7]

Is this not true in the church also? We see the changes taking place around us. We may even appreciate the changes as long as they do not mean we have to change, too.

As mentioned before, coauthor Glen Martin likes to say that some leaders are risk takers, some are caretakers, and others are undertakers. For a church to be effective in our changing times, church leaders need to be risk takers. Allow staff and volunteers to experiment with new ideas. Redefine failure by asking all staff, leaders, and volunteers to try at least five ministry experiments during the year. Tell them you expect them to have three experiments fail. And, of course, that is okay since some experiments always fail. Remember: the best fruit is always out on a limb.

▼

NOTES

[1] Alvin Toffler, *Future Shock* (New York: Bantam Books, 1970), 143.

[2] Quoted by Barbara H. Peters and James Peters in "Corporate Leadership for a Changing West," in *Business Week* (March 29, 1993) n. a.

[3] "The Most Successful Ad in History," *Success* (February 1993), 18.

[4] Advertisement in *Fortune,* (November 30, 1992), 52.

[5] Adapted from "Rivalry in the Fire Department" by Leon Davis published in the FEDCO Reporter, June 1993.

[6] Thomas J. Watson, quoted by Anna Esaki-Smith in "Fighters," *Success* (August 1992), 22.

[7] Ueberroth, Peter. Quoted in "Corporate Leadership for a Changing West," in *Business Week* (March 29, 1993), n. a.

RESOURCES

Tapes:

George, Carl F. and Logan, Robert E. *How to Lead and Manage the Local Church.* Available from the Charles E. Fuller Association, P. O. Box 91990, Pasadena, CA 91109-1990; (800) 999-9578.

Manuals:

Gottschalk, R. Michael. *The Complete Guidebook to Church Hiring.*

McIntosh, Gary L. *How to Develop a Pastoral Compensation Plan.*

McIntosh, Gary L. *How to Develop a Policy Manual.*

Lacy, Walt. *How to Supervise Church Staff and Volunteers.*

All available from the Church Growth Institute, P. O. Box 4404, Lynchburg, VA 24502; (800) 553-GROW.

For Further Reading:

Arn, Win. *The Church Growth Ratio Book.* Pasadena, Calif.: Church Growth Press, 1987.

Callahan, Kennon L. *Twelve Keys to an Effective Church: Strategic Planning for Mission.* San Francisco: Harper & Row, 1983.

George, Carl F. and Logan, Robert E. *Leading and Managing Your Church.* Old Tappan, N. J.: Fleming H. Revell, 1987.

Hemphill, Ken. *The Bonsai Theory of Church Growth.* Nashville: Broadman Press, 1991.

Logan, Robert E. *Beyond Church Growth.* Old Tappan, N. J.: Fleming H. Revell, 1989.

Schaller, Lyle E. *Choices for Churches.* Nashville: Abingdon, 1990.

6

First man: "We've been declining for some time now."
Second man: "Yes. What do you think we can do about it?"
First: "I think if we hired a youth pastor it would help."
Second: "I agree. Our pastor doesn't seem to relate well with youth."
First: "So I've noticed."
Second: "Let's talk to the board. What we need is a youth pastor."
—Overheard in a conversation between two men in a local church

STAFFING

Laetrile is a colorless liquid pressed from the soft, bitter outside of apricot pits. In Sweden, you can buy the stuff in the grocery store for about the price of almond extract, and you use it in baking, much as you would any other extract. In Mexico, you can buy it for fifty dollars a drop to "cure" your fatal cancer. Of course, it does not cure anything. All evidence demonstrates that it is a cruel fraud, but since no one else has anything to offer, terminal patients accept the claims of the laetrile peddlers, no matter how outrageous. People who are desperate do not look carefully at the evidence.

Similarly, many church leaders are "desperate enough" to become victims of the symbolic laetrile that is being proposed as "the answer" to your staffing needs—hire a youth pastor.

Historically, staffing a church was never much of an issue. It has only been since the beginning of the industrial age, which began in the late 1800s, that enough people were gathered in cities and churches to create a need for multiple church staff.

In the first half of the twentieth century, not many churches were large enough to need multiple staff. Most church ministries were carried on by volunteers such as the youth sponsor, the Sunday School superintendent, and the visitation committee. After World War II, as churches responded to the growth of their congregation, staffing became a realistic need. The birth rates of the early fifties and sixties produced the largest generation ever in the United States. The baby boomers hit our churches in such large numbers that volunteer staff could not take care of the rush. This was especially felt as this generation hit the teenage years in 1959. Youth ministry became the issue, and the simple solution to staffing needs was to hire a youth pastor.

But that was then and this is now. Staffing is no longer solved through such easy solutions. The times have changed, and so have trends for staffing a growing church.

Trends in Staffing

On a flight to Orlando, Florida, in 1992, Glen grew increasingly aware of the number of ads in the on-flight reading that claimed to boost sales, productivity, and output by 100 percent or more. During his five-hour flight, he accumulated quite a pile. The diversity of methodology was amazing. There were seminars, packaged programs, and newsletters. If you could name it, it was available. The final ad that he spotted was on the back of the New

Staffing

That was then...	This is now...
▲ Generalists	▲ Specialists
▲ Broad spectrum	▲ Departmentalized
▲ 1 pastor/300 attendance	▲ 1 pastor/150 attendance
▲ Pastoral counseling	▲ Pastor of counseling
▲ Church secretary	▲ Executive secretary
▲ Pastoral visitation	▲ Pastor of visitation
▲ Competitive ministry	▲ Team ministry
▲ Administrative help	▲ Pastor of administration
▲ Job requirements	▲ Ministry descriptions
▲ Unspoken expectations	▲ Performance objectives
▲ Staff as employees	▲ Staff as associates
▲ Single pastor	▲ Multiple staff
▲ Flying solo	▲ Flying in formation
▲ Staff hired on feelings	▲ Staff hired on giftedness

York *Post*. It read, "Lose Weight While Sleeping." Perfect! We all want "the answer" but wish to avoid the work involved.

1. Purpose Based Staffing

Hiring staff is no longer a shot in the dark for church leaders. Today's church leaders select staff based on the purpose of their church with an eye on which position will help them accomplish their stated goals.

Personality testing assists churches in choosing staff who will complement their current pastors and build the best team for the long haul. Some of the more popular testing tools are the Performax DISC Test, the LEAD Personality Inventory, and the Role Preference Inventory.[1]

2. Professional Support Staff

Growing churches understand the need to provide support staff as well as pastoral staff. Support staff includes janitors, maintenance personnel, interns, paid sponsors, secretaries, and other administrative help. While a minimum ratio is one support person for every two pastoral staff, the growing complexity of our society is pushing this ratio to a one-to-one comparison.

Recognizing that professional support staff are a viable part of a successful team, churches give equal care to hiring support staff as they do for pastoral staff. Support staff are chosen on the basis of competence. Secretaries no longer simply answer phones and do a little typing. They are professionals who are computer literate, competent in communication, superb managers of people, and committed to the purpose and vision of the church.

3. Greater Staff Accountability

Expectations for ministry performance are higher than ever before. Church leaders and regular attenders look for churches that demonstrate excellence in all aspects of ministry. The days of keeping a staff person on payroll, even when he is not doing the job, are rapidly passing us by.

In place of unspoken expectations, church leaders write ministry performance objectives in conjunction with each staff person. Ministry objectives written after consultation between leaders, the senior pastor, and other staff members serve as a motivation for ministry. Performance objectives are reviewed on a quarterly time schedule in an effort to keep communication lines open.

4. Senior Pastor Hires Own Staff

As part of the trend to simplify decision making, churches delegate authority to senior pastors to hire and fire their own staff with ratification from the church board.

Building a team of pastors and support personnel who are committed to the purpose and vision of the church means someone must communicate the dream. In 99.9 percent of the cases, that person is the senior pastor. Additional staff are selected to fit into the team led by the senior pastor; thus, the senior pastor exercises authority to select the team.

5. Staff Given Responsibility and Authority

One of the difficulties in building a staff team is balancing responsibility with authority. It is unfair, let alone unproductive, to give a staff person responsibility while withholding the necessary authority to get the job done.

Growing churches find it best to select competent staff, give them responsibility to do their ministry, and delegate to them the commensurate authority to do it. Instead of placing a staff person under a committee which often strangles and negates performance, staff people are set free to do the job. If assistance is needed, they have the authority to form a task force to help accomplish their objectives. They then are the leaders of the task force, rather than being followers of an ineffective committee.

6. Stress Team Building

Marc Lory is a forty-four-year-old expert mountaineer. He has climbed Mount McKinley and Mount Everest. As the founder of Orlux Distribution Inc., an eyewear distribution company in Santa Ana, California, he is one of the top entrepreneurs in southern California. "Mountains are climbed in teams where every member is an essential link to reaching the goal," he explains. "It doesn't matter if you have the best climber in the world on your team. If you have one weak link, the whole team will fall."[2] Growing churches focus on building a smoothly functioning team with high commitment to the church's vision, rather than promoting stars.

7. Increased Staff Ratios

At mid-century the ratio of pastoral staff to worship attendance was about one pastor for every three hundred people. This ratio was adequate for a time when churches had a simple structure and the needs of people were not as complex as they are today.

As the personal needs of people became more complex, the ratio changed to one pastor for every 150 people in the church. Today, with the explosion of dysfunctional families and related issues, churches with a traditional model of staffing need one pastor for every one hundred people.

Ideas for Staffing

The growing complexity of the information age made it nearly impossible for a single pastor to deal with all the issues and needs of people. As the secular world moves toward specialization and subspecialization, so the church is responding with ministry specialization to meet people's complex needs.

1. Staff for Growth

Observers of growing churches find that the best years for a church's numerical growth are often the first fifteen to twenty years of its existence. One of the reasons for this rapid growth in the early years of a church's history is related to its priorities.

The typical church organizes around six main areas of ministry: evangelism, assimilation, worship, education, administration and care. Using slightly different terms, these priorities are illustrated below.

Areas and Priorities of Ministry					
Priority in early years			Priority in later years		
Find New People	Keep New People	Celebrate with People	Educate the People	Oversee the People	Care for People

In the early years of a church's ministry, the priority is on the left side of the continuum. As the church grows, the priority shifts to the right. Essentially, a church moves from an outreach mode into a maintenance mode, taking care of what it has (people, programs, and facilities) and abandoning the priorities that got it there in the first place (finding, keeping, and worshiping).

The tendency of most churches is to call staff to serve the priorities on the right side of the continuum. Ultimately, staffing the right side leads to an ingrown church, taking care of its own, but neglecting the finding and keeping of newer people.

Growing churches call staff to serve priorities on the left side of the continuum. Staff who help find new people (evangelism), keep new people (assimilation), and lead worship (celebration) focus efforts on priorities that result in continued growth.

All of the six areas of ministry are necessary to provide a supportive environment for church growth. However, churches wanting to reach their greatest potential will place a higher emphasis on the priorities of the left. Staff your church for growth by serving the functions of ministry on the left of the continuum before those areas on the right side.

2. Invest in Training

Training is the most powerful tool senior pastors and church leaders can use to build mutual commitment and create a productive staff team.

Train staff in the basic functions of their ministry. Small errors or omissions in basic training create big administrative headaches. Newer staff benefit from training by quickly learning the ropes. They feel more comfortable and competent in handling routine responsibilities. Older staff set the example by participating in ongoing training events where they can pass along some of their skills to younger staff.

Since people learn in different ways, offer training through a variety of means. Some will easily absorb and digest written policies while others need more of a "hands-on" approach where modeling is provided. Whatever training method is chosen, the key ingredient is the systematic monitoring and feedback to the staff member. Never wait until a staff member's progress is hampered before sharing input concerning his or her growth. Frequent communication and accountability early in the training process are most successful in building a team spirit.

Cross train staff to function in different roles. Bo Jackson is not the only one who can play two sports. Assist staff in identifying their gift mix so that they can cross over to other areas of ministry when there is a need. Communicate a broader vision of team effectiveness whereby everyone works together to make each other successful.

Train staff to be responsible. Professional staff do not want to be shackled with too many controls. Over-control erodes initiative and commitment. It frequently fosters passive dependence and irresponsibility. Simply put, proper training produces workers who can act independently, exercise self-control, and initiate constructive suggestions for the overall vision. Successful training requires both controlling and releasing of staff in ministry.

3. Give Staff Appropriate Authority

Allow staff the authority to do their ministry. Resist placing staff under a committee or other board that uses a "NO" permission system and destroys motivation.[3] The reverse should be employed whenever possible: give responsibility and authority to one person and let that person recruit a team to assist in getting the job done.

Set up reporting lines so that staff report to one person who is on-site full-time, usually a senior staff person. In no case ask a staff person to report to a committee or more than one person.

Allow each staff person to establish his or her own performance objectives individually with a senior staff person. Be certain each has the authority necessary to carry out his or her plans.

4. Encourage Professional Growth

Require staff to actively pursue continuing education. Expect them to spend a minimum of ten contact hours in workshops or seminars per year. Ask all staff to read a minimum of four books a year. Support your expectations by providing each staff with at least 1 percent of their salary for the purchase of books, magazines, and newsletter subscriptions.

Support for growth and change must be cultivated long before the growth actually occurs, very much as a gardener would go out and till his soil, fertilize, weed, and even water the seedlings before he could expect any fruit to grow. Growing churches have growing leadership, and growth begins with the pastoral staff keeping current in their specialized ministry areas.

5. Prepare Your Staff for Growth

Growth rises and falls on the competence of leadership. Giving people work and responsibility without training them and giving them the opportunity to develop is just asking for trouble. In order for people development to keep pace with church development, pastors and key leaders must continually look ahead to forecast and act out expectations. To help accomplish this, develop the staff team by anticipating the specific areas staff need to grow in and by utilizing seminars or workshops which relate to those needs.

6. Grow a Team

What we need is a shift from team building to team growing. This is less of a technological image and more of an agricultural image. Agriculture is not entirely controllable. We enrich the soil, plant seeds, water according to the latest theory or process, and then hold our breath. It just might grow; then, it may not. That is pretty close to how team formation works.

However, there are ways to increase the chances that staff will bond together. Since people bond as they spend time together, each year schedule two staff retreats. At the first retreat review your church's purpose and vision, noting how each staff member fits into the total picture. Then work together on the coming year's plans. Schedule the second retreat about six months later and have each staff member bring his or her spouse. Use this retreat for developing relationships among the members. Try to provide office space that houses staff members together. Practice an open door policy and visit every staff member in his or her office on a casual basis.

7. Build Confidence

A large church in California called upon us to identify some of their staffing inadequacies. They were, in fact, over-staffed, having a pastor for every 100-120 people in their church. Their structure was well organized, and the pastor was a visionary. Externally, everything was there for a well-oiled machine—except trust. The staff was not given freedom to try anything new. Only the senior pastor's judgment was competent, and everyone else's was suspect. The result: teamicide.

We cannot protect our team from failures; but once we've decided to go with a given group, the best tactic is to trust them. There is no defensive measure that will guarantee success. Over-control may give short-term peace of mind, but will poison any chance of the team growing.

8. Eliminate Excess Paperwork

Mindless paperwork is a waste. It needs to be attacked because, unknowingly, it keeps people from working. This red tape hinders team growth.

While we all need to be held accountable, long reports can often stifle staff effectiveness. After all, job descriptions change. In today's changing climate, ministry is dynamic, not static. So flexibility is a must. Here are a few suggestions to decrease paper work.

▲ Change your thinking from job descriptions to performance objectives. What are the standards by which you will measure staff performance, not simply cover your bases?

▲ Perform performance reviews twice a year. The senior pastor, or executive pastor as seen in many larger churches, must personalize the review process by individually evaluating progress.

▲ Maintain simple weekly reports.
This format will not take much time and will provide enough information to evaluate progress and performance weekly.

Weekly Report

Information Items (ministry updates for our information only)

_____

_____

_____

Study Items (issues you would like discussed for input only)

_____

_____

_____

Action Items (issues you need a decision on)

_____

_____

_____

Prayer Items (How can we be praying for you specifically?)

_____

_____

_____

Name _____

Lastly, eliminate minutes from staff meetings. An agenda is more than sufficient to keep track of programming needs.

9. Make Ministry Rewarding

The best way to accomplish this task appears to be recognition. Weekly, or at least quarterly, recognize a staff member at your staff meeting with a small present. Frequently express thanks for specific jobs they have done well. Each year host a special banquet for staff members and their families where you recognize their commitment, sacrifice, and work. Budget 1 percent of the total church budget to give as end-of-the-year bonuses to faithful staff members. Allow the senior pastor to give the bonuses to the pastoral staff under his oversight.

Everyone yearns to be a significant part of the future. As a leader, do not be afraid to describe how you foresee the church many years down the road and what part each staff member will play in that future.

10. Make a Commitment to Excellence

People who work together must have a long-term commitment and vision to stick with each other and the organization through all the short-term discomforts of growth and change. It will take this kind of commitment to stick together through the growing pains in the church. If long-term commitments cannot be generated, inevitably turnover occurs and pastors begin again the long and costly process of starting over with a new staff member or recruit.

Commitment cannot be created in the middle of a growth spurt. Commitment begins the moment a pastor and staff join hands. It will either grow or diminish from that point on.

Some baseball fans complain about the sorry state of the game today. They reach out for the nostalgia of former years when players played for the sake of the game rather than for the money. Whether things were as pure in the old days as these fans would like us to imagine, we do not honestly know. However, in our saner moments, we do know that the old days are gone forever. We live in changing times, and baseball is not likely to return to the days of peanuts and Cracker Jacks.

In a similar manner, some people remember the days when one pastor would take care of everything. Whether it was preaching, marrying, or burying, we could always count on having the same pastor by our side. Whether these "good old days" were really that good, we do not know. But in our saner moments, we do know that those days are likely gone forever. We live in changing times, and staffing a church is not likely to return to the days of the jack-of-all-trades pastor.

▼

NOTES

[1] For information on these inventories, see the resource section for chapter 4, Leadership.

[2] Quoted by Jenny C. McCune in "Train Your Team to Scale New Heights," *Success* (June 1992), 25.

[3] See chapter 5 for a complete description of a YES permission system.

RESOURCES

Tapes:

Mentoring: How to Find a Mentor and How to Become One. Available from Masterplanning Group International, Box 6128, Laguna Hills, CA 92607; (800) 443-1976.

For Further Reading:

Arn, Win. *The Church Growth Ratio Book.* Pasadena, Calif.: Church Growth Press, 1987.

Brown, Jerry. *Church Staff Teams That Win.* Nashville: Convention Press, 1979.

George, Carl F. *How to Break Growth Barriers.* Grand Rapids, Mich.: Baker Book House, 1993.

Schaller, Lyle E. *The Multiple Staff and the Larger Church.* Nashville: Abingdon Press, 1980.

Schaller, Lyle E. *Getting Things Done.* Nashville: Abingdon Press, 1986.

Westing, Harold. *Multiple Church Staff Handbook.* Grand Rapids, Mich.: Kregel Publications, 1985.

7

*Christians and non-Christians have something in common,
we're both uptight about evangelism.*
 —Rebecca Pippert

*Lift up your eyes, and look on the fields,
that they are white for harvest.*
 —John 4:35, NASB

OUTREACH

Gary did not like to be disturbed on Sunday morning. His normal routine was to get up late, eat a large breakfast with his grandmother, then settle down to watch the Game of the Week. Sports was his major interest, not church.

For weeks he was disturbed each Sunday morning as his best friend would come to invite him to attend Sunday School in a nearby church. What Gary did not realize was that the teacher of the class, a single lady in her late sixties, was encouraging her class to invite their friends to Sunday School.

Gary would hear his grandmother answer the door and, in a sad voice, say, "I'm sorry, honey. Gary didn't get up again. Maybe he'll go next week." Fortunately, Gary's best friend didn't give up. Due to his friend's constant invitations, Gary finally got up one morning and went to Sunday School.

The class was typical of junior high Sunday School classes found in churches of the fifties and sixties. The students gathered in an opening session, after which they went to their individual classes. The junior high class began with singing from a tattered hymn book, followed by announcements and the welcoming of new students. This lasted for about half an hour after which the teacher would lead in a Bible lesson from a quarterly book.

While students learned much about the Bible, the underlying reason for the class was not education, but evangelism. At the end of every lesson, the teacher would explain the gospel message, ask the students to close their eyes, and to raise their hands if they would like to receive Christ as their Savior.

Gary had resisted going to Sunday School for years. But this time he came back a second and then a third time. The third week when the teacher asked who would like to pray to receive Christ, Gary raised his hand. He's been involved in church ever since.

Many Christians older than forty-five years old can identify with the Sunday School approach that reached Gary. Mention the word "evangelism" and they would know exactly what you meant. Hand out tracts, *The Roman Road*, invite your friends to Sunday School, preach at the local mission, attend the Youth for Christ Saturday Night Rally, host a yearly revival, sponsor a Vacation Bible School, and go door-to-door in the church neighborhood. These were outreach methods effective in bringing people to personal faith in Jesus Christ.

But that was then and this is now.

Outreach

That was then...	This is now...
▲ Door-to-door	▲ Friend-to-friend
▲ Confrontational	▲ Relational
▲ Tracts	▲ Multimedia
▲ Hard sell	▲ Soft sell
▲ Yearly revivals	▲ Ongoing life-style
▲ Evangelistic Bible study	▲ Twelve step groups
▲ Event-oriented	▲ Process-oriented
▲ Evangelism committees	▲ Evangelism teams
▲ Guilt driven	▲ Love driven
▲ Altar calls	▲ Response cards
▲ Evangelism a duty	▲ Evangelism a life-style
▲ Basic Bible knowledge	▲ Limited Bible knowledge
▲ Christian belief system	▲ Pluralistic belief system
▲ Social networks intact	▲ Social networks broken
▲ People were sociable	▲ People resist socializing
▲ Emphasis on outreach	▲ Emphasis on education

In the second half of this century, significant changes have taken place which have relegated many of these highly regarded evangelism methods of the past to ineffectiveness at the least. After five years of research, Dr. Charles Arn wrote in 1986: "Today 'evangelism'—as widely practiced in American churches—is inhibiting the fulfillment of the Great Commission!"[1] A startling statement which, we're certain, many will disagree with strongly. Yet, to be ruthlessly honest, we must admit that evangelism in most churches is not as effective as it once was. While the basic need of people remains the same—to know Christ as their personal Savior—our changing world demands new approaches to win people to Christ.

Outreach Trends

Methods of evangelism have changed over the years. In the middle 1800s the trend was the camp meeting. A Norwegian immigrant, Mrs. Elise Waerenskjold, visited a camp meeting in Texas and called it the "oddest form of Christian worship." But for at least three generations, camp meetings were the most significant method for evangelism carried on in the southern frontier areas of the United States.

A typical camp meeting lasted for ten days or more. Most were held in forest areas where wood, shade, and a stream or other supply of water could be found for people, horses, and mules.

Entire families would come together often housed in tents. Meals were cooked on outdoor fires. During the preaching, heavy boards or logs served as seats, over which an arbor of tree limbs was often erected. The encampments varied from several hundred to several thousand people.

The day typically began at 5:00 A.M. for prayer, with breakfast at 7:00 followed by preaching and worship which lasted all morning. Lunch was at noon with another session of preaching until supper at 5:00 P.M. After supper there was still another session of preaching until late in the evening.

Camp meetings undoubtedly served a useful function. Besides bringing many hundreds, perhaps thousands to Christ, they served as social gatherings for isolated pioneer families who were starving for social contacts.[2]

Camp meetings met essential needs in the late 1800s and on into the early 1900s. But with the changing of society, they eventually were replaced by other methods of evangelism that fit the context of a new day.

Today most church leaders would not even consider using the camp meeting approach to evangelism. It is obvious that it was a method for an earlier time in North American history. But what are the "camp meetings" for today? What are the trends in evangelism that God is using to win people to Christ in our changing society? The following are five trends we have observed.

1. Target Groups

Mark Galli, an associate editor of *Leadership,* visited several churches which were successfully reaching new people for Christ, only to find a baffling variety of outreach methodologies. Struggling to define some clear principles of evangelistically effective churches, he determined that "each church I examined has decided that it cannot be all things to all people. In one way or another, each has determined its unique identity as well as whom it is able to reach."[3]

Today's evangelistically successful churches do not ignore Christ's message to go "into all the world" (Matt. 28:19), but they do believe effective use of their resources demands that they carefully select those who will be most responsive to their presentation of the gospel. The issue is one of choosing a clear priority for the use of limited resources: people, time, and money. Designing outreach events and programming for clearly defined groups of people produces better results than approaches aimed at broader audiences. "Instead of pretending they exist to serve everyone," wrote Lyle Schaller, "these churches have carved out a specialized niche in ministry and seek to excel in that specialized role."[4] Since the result of trying to be all things to all people often results in being nothing to anyone, Schaller continued, "Evangelism in the nineties is niche. You pick out a segment, a slice of the market you want to try to reach, and develop a ministry for that slice."[5]

2. Church Advertising

A basic question all churches must ask is "What do people outside our church think about us?" In all cases there are only three possible answers:

1. They think of our church positively.
2. They think of our church negatively.
3. They don't think of our church at all!

Answer number one creates an environment for effective outreach. Answer number two is a tragedy. Answer number three is anathema! Today's church seeks to create an environment where people do think of their church and think of it positively.

New Testament churches, of course, never had a brochure or direct mail campaign; however, they did create an atmosphere where growth occurred. Often the means they used were what we today would call advertising. The personal letters of the New Testament are an obvious medium—direct mail—in our terms. Peter and Paul used this advertising tool to communicate their love, care, teachings, and exhortation to people who could not be reached in any other way. Word-of-mouth advertising was instrumental in reaching unchurched people around Thessalonica. "The word of the Lord has sounded [echoed] forth from you," stated Paul, "not only in Macedonia and Achaia, but also in every place your faith toward God has gone forth, so that we have no need to say anything" (1 Thess. 1:8, NASB).

Growing churches tend to rely primarily on word-of-mouth advertising to attract people. Other forms of advertising build an awareness of a church in its community. Advertising a church's ministry reaches people where they live and attracts many to attend church where they are exposed to the gospel.[6]

3. Support Groups

It all began in the sixties. The confusion of the Vietnam War, the disillusionment of Watergate, and the loss of hope arising from the assassinations of John F. Kennedy, Martin Luther King, Jr., and Robert Kennedy led many young people to try to anesthetize their internal pain. LSD, marijuana, other mind-altering drugs, and free sex covered the hurt for some for a time. The trusted morals and institutions which had guided the previous generation were discarded for a secular MEism and a "let it all hang out" and "anything goes" approach to life.

The long-term result was an extremely large number of dysfunctional people. The list of hurting people goes on and on. Bill Perkins, in *Fatal Attractions,* gave the following six general categories of addictions covering deeper hurts being felt by people: eating disorders, sexual addictions, codependencies, exercise, negativism, and workaholism. Think of the times you have heard about people facing the following issues in just the last year: bulimia, anorexia, or obesity; extramarital affairs; sexual exploitation of children and teenagers (boys and girls); prostitution; mental, physical, verbal, or sexual abuse; alcohol, nicotine, caffeine, pornography, and work addiction; excessive involvement in running, aerobics, skiing, or other sports activities; overly controlling pessimistic attitudes, words, thoughts, and behaviors. No doubt you have heard of political leaders, athletes, religious leaders, and even some of your own friends, perhaps even church members, who have faced some of these issues.

Of course, every generation has had its share of hurts. But what makes our era so different is the sheer number of "fatal attractions" being observed in people. Unchurched people are facing life with deep feelings of anger, loneliness, frustration, disillusionment, shame, unworthiness, hate, guilt, and disappointment.

Is it any wonder that the most effective way of reaching the unchurched for Christ today is support group ministries? Churches find that offering various need-meeting support groups draws people into loving environments where they receive healing for their emotional hurts, overcome their "fatal attractions" and receive the good news of salvation in Christ Jesus.[7]

4. Team Evangelism

The two words that bring the most fear to church members are *evangelism* and *witnessing*. Just the mention of these words arouses feelings of fear and failure in the minds of the average church member. These words cause experienced Christians to envision standing at the door of a home they do not recognize and getting ready to talk to a person they do not know about the most important decision they will ever be asked to make—in a few short minutes!

In an effort to develop a better approach to outreach, churches have found that teaming people with other Christians effectively uses the special giftedness of each one in a cooperative effort to win people to Christ. It also eliminates the me-against-the-world feeling often associated with evangelism.

A good example of this new team approach to outreach is that of Wayne Gordon, pastor of Lawndale Community Church in urban Chicago. He divides the team this way:

▲ Plowers: People who get the soil ready by helping neighbors and building friendships.

▲ Planters: People who plant an initial understanding of the gospel by sharing some of the message of Christ.

▲ Cultivators: People who weed, fertilize, and water by living godly, attractive lives.

▲ Reapers: People who harvest the crop by leading others to personal faith in Christ.[8]

This new outreach ministry model respects the individual personalities, talents, and gifts of each person by not forcing people into the role of reaper. It recognizes that everyone is to be a "witness" (Acts 1:8) without expecting all to be "evangelists" (Eph. 4:11–12).

5. Multimedia

People in their mid-forties and below have been raised on television. They are visually oriented, have attention spans of about thirty seconds, and are united by a common "electronic" bond. Books, tracts, and other written material have lost some of their power for evangelism since the younger generations are scanners rather than readers.

In response to the visual nature of the younger generations, some churches are hiring staff members to develop videos for announcements, mission programs, visitation, and training. Providing video is also a way to reach unchurched individuals in their normal patterns of life. People who may not come to a church event will listen and watch Christian messages on video in their own homes on their chosen time schedule.

Increasing Outreach in Changing Times

While the basic need of people remains the same—to know Christ as their personal Savior—our changing world demands new approaches to win people to Christ. We suggest you implement some of the following ideas.

1. Build an Evangelism Consciousness

The heartbeat of an outreaching church will be that of Christ's—to seek and save the lost! A church without this basic consciousness will have difficulty in reaching out to new people. To raise the evangelism consciousness of your church, teach the basics of salvation on a regular basis. Be certain to communicate a desire for outreach in your church's overall purpose and vision. Call attention to the needs of unchurched people in your community. For example, Bear Valley Community Church, located in a Denver suburb, took all worshipers on a tour of its community in order to expose them to the needs of unchurched people.

2. Pray for People's Salvation

When church members hear their leaders praying for unbelievers, they will desire to pray for their own unchurched friends. Begin praying for the salvation of people you know. As appropriate, pray publicly for the salvation of people in a general way. In smaller groups pray specifically for friends or neighbors to set the model for other members of your church. Encourage members to pray for unchurched friends. Some churches encourage members to make yearly prayer lists of unchurched people they know. Those who desire make a personal commitment to pray for a friend's salvation for an entire year. Lists are often turned in so that church leaders can pray with the church members during the year.

3. Create Name Recognition

Unchurched people often do not have a high respect for churches. Growing churches have found that they need to create an environment where unchurched people think of their church positively. If your church is not well known in your ministry area, or perhaps has a less than positive image, it will be important to spend time and money in creating better name recognition.

Advertising your church's ministry to your target audience is one way to accomplish this purpose. Mailing a brochure about your church to homes in your ministry area is a good way to begin. Called a "first impression piece," such a brochure gives you the opportunity to communicate the benefits of your ministry to people who need what you have to offer. Consider creating a professionally designed first impression piece for your church. The first year mail it to all homes within a three-mile radius of your church. The next year mail it to all homes within a five-mile radius and so on until you have covered your entire ministry area.

4. Identify Your Primary Target

Churches which are effective in reaching people for Christ have identified their target audience(s) and designed programs for that particular group of people. We like to think that our church is able to reach anyone for Christ. In some cases, God does uniquely gift a local church with a wide ministry; but usually, a single local church has a fairly narrow target group of reachable people.

Develop a list of the various groups of unreached people in your community, noting some specific felt needs. Then evaluate which group(s) God has gifted you to reach. "We analyze our community over and over and over—more than we do ourselves," said Doug Muren, pastor of Eastside Foursquare Church, Kirkland, Washington, in an article in *Leadership.* "We analyze it demographically and psychographically. We've found out, for instance, that there are over ten thousand single moms in our community, within five miles of us. That radically changed how we addressed outreach."[9]

5. Profile the Unchurched in Your Area

Churches which reach new people for Christ understand the characteristics, values, and life-styles of the unchurched in their target area and develop ministries which communicate the good news of Jesus Christ in ways the unchurched understand. To start, develop a profile of the typical unchurched person you might meet at a local restaurant. For example, Glen led his church, Community Baptist Church of Manhattan Beach, California, to develop a profile of "Community Cathy and Carl." They then listed eleven characteristics of Cathy and Carl.

Characteristics of Community Cathy and Carl

1. High level of education.
2. Desire job satisfaction.
3. Love the South Bay.
4. Committed to fitness.
5. Rather be in a large group than a small one.
6. Skeptical of organized religion.
7. Enjoy contemporary music.
8. Afraid about tomorrow.
9. Both have to work.
10. Prefer the casual to the formal.
11. Over-extended in time and money.

---

6. Design Presence Evangelism Events

An outreaching church does not expect the unchurched to come to them. Instead they develop presence among their target group(s) in a minimum of three ways. A church which wants to reach its community for Christ will begin at least one new ministry each year which will meet a specific need of a specific group of people. For example, one church discovered a need for and started an AIDS support group for parents of AIDS victims. Other churches have begun presence ministries, such as sports teams, basic automobile repair classes, craft programs, and similar events.

7. Emphasize Training

Evangelism has a visible place in churches which win people to Christ. As a rule, growing churches tend to highlight outreach by regularly training members—often, a minimum of 10 percent of their people each year in some form of outreach ministry.

In our book *Finding Them, Keeping Them* we noted that evangelism training should deal with the three levels of planting, cultivating, and harvesting found in 1 Corinthians 3:5–9. A church should train 80 percent of its people to be planters who simply invite friends to church events where they may be exposed to Christian values and God's Word. Following this should be outreach training which focuses on cultivating relationships with unchurched people. Often called "friendship" or "lifestyle" evangelism, this form of outreach takes more time and personal investment. Typically, only about 50 percent will have the personality traits to be cultivators. Finally, a church should invest outreach training into harvesting, or what has traditionally been called "soul

Levels of Evangelism

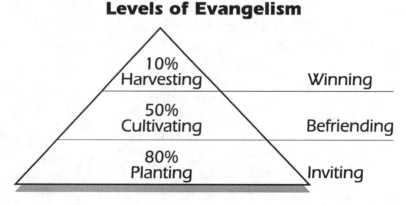

10% Harvesting — Winning

50% Cultivating — Befriending

80% Planting — Inviting

winning." God has gifted about 10 percent to be successful at leading the unchurched into a personal relationship with Christ.[10]

8. Focus on Relationships

General Motors Corporation once asked thousands of car buyers what they hated most about shopping for a car. The number one answer was haggling over the price. Why was this so important to know? Because car salesmen typically spend 25 percent of their time showing the car to customers and 75 percent of their time negotiating. So, when GM introduced Saturn, the car with the special mission of converting buyers of Japanese cars to GM, the company decided to reinvent the process of selling cars. Saturn dealers are called "retailers"; to eliminate haggling, at most dealerships the sticker price is fixed and there are no sales commissions. The Saturn customer is handled with a deference unheard of in the auto industry: he is allowed to roam the dealership until he is finished examining the goods. At its Spring Hill, Tennessee, headquarters, the company trains retailers to lower the pressure and to provide service that creates good word of mouth. And Saturn is selling cars faster than it can make them. In 1992, some 196,000 Saturns were sold, and the company is shooting for 300,000 in 1993.

Now we clearly do not get our direction from General Motors, but the trend away from "hard sell" to "soft sell" is applicable to our understanding of effective evangelism. The "grab 'em and stab 'em" approach to outreach is gone. Today it is more helpful to "hug 'em and love 'em." Confrontation with the gospel must take place within the context of a relationship of love and mutual respect. God wants us also to obey His second greatest commandment: love your neighbor as yourself. Most of us would want to be dealt with in a highly respectful manner.

9. Try Something New

Nothing works forever. The general consensus is that prepackaged outreach training programs have a useful life of about three to five years. The first two years tend to provide the most results with a slight decline in the years following. Continually testing new ideas is a real benefit.

Zig Ziglar wrote in *Ziglar on Selling:* "The profession of selling soon teaches you that people do things for their reason, not yours." Focus on the needs of the people that you know. Why do they need

Christ? What would be the need in their life right now which may be an open door to present the gospel?

Consider the following open doors for outreach. Which ones could you design a new outreach ministry around this year?

Birth of a child. New parents are concerned with the physical and spiritual needs of raising children. Often, young parents will come back to church to give their children a spiritual upbringing.

Times of crisis. Times of crisis such as death, sickness, and job loss cause people to consider the major issues of life. What is the purpose of life? Why did this happen to me? What do I do now? are some of the questions people ask.

Following a move. Our mobile society destroys the natural networks of friendships. People moving into a new housing area are searching for friends, doctors, dentists, places to shop, and churches.

After Divorce. Churches are finding one of the main opportunities for reaching people with the gospel is through divorce recovery workshops. The large number of marriages ending in divorce is not likely to let up in the coming years. Alert churches will establish ministries among this hurting group.

Times of Hurt. Drug, mental, sexual, and physical abuse have taken an emotional toll on many people. The support group movement is a response to this situation and effective churches are developing new ministries to meet the needs of abused people.

Physical Fitness. Participation in fitness centers, spas, golf, walking, jogging, and other forms of sports and recreation is on the rise. Reaching the unchurched through various athletic programs is a ministry opportunity many churches should explore.

Single Parenting. The number of single parents is increasing in the United States. Creative churches are starting new ministries aimed at this receptive target group. Support groups and classes on single parenting are some of the most common.

Interest in the Arts. As public schools cut back on band and choral music programs, some churches are discovering an opportunity to reach their communities by offering lessons in the arts.

Child Care. The continuing increase in the number of two-income families and single parents creates a need for child care. Preschools and child care centers will likely be a ministry churches will use in reaching their unchurched communities.

10. Make Heroes of People

Who are the heroes in your church? We have discovered that for most churches the category of hero falls upon those who serve in the kitchen. Think back to a recent church dinner where the kitchen was staffed with faithful volunteers. What ritual took place following the dinner? If your church is like many, the cooks were encouraged to come out of the kitchen while the people who ate the meal applauded them. Sound familiar? They are the heroes!

The question is "When do we applaud those who win others to Christ?"

Not often, in many churches. Our members and regular attenders learn quickly what is important in our church—serving in the kitchen! We are not putting down those faithful servants who serve tables, but we also need to raise up those who are seeking and saving the lost. Consider the following ideas and pick an appropriate one for your church.

▲ Allow those who win another person to Christ to baptize or at least be in the baptismal waters with the person they won to Christ.

▲ Interview people being baptized or being received into membership by asking them to name the people who were instrumental in their coming to Christ.

▲ After people are named above, ask them to stand and have the congregation applaud them.

▲ Twice a year host an appreciation dinner for everyone who has had any part in bringing another person to Christ.

▲ Once a year hand out a friendship award to everyone in your church who has participated in winning another to Christ.

Perhaps the classic presence evangelism story comes from a Friends Church which started a very unique ministry in the late 1970s. A survey of younger families in the church's ministry area revealed that the main need of young mothers was information on how to potty train their children. So a "Potty Training Course" for young mothers was started which became a contact point for salvation in Christ for many younger families and, for many, an entry point into that church.

Many of the methods which won people to Christ in past days are not seeing great results today. Churches which are serious about doing their part to win people to Christ in the years ahead of us will need to use the same creativity as this Friends Church.

▼

NOTES

[1] W. Charles Arn, "Evangelism or Disciple Making?" in *Church Growth State of the Art* (Wheaton, Ill.: Tyndale House Publishers, Inc., 1986), 57.

[2] Walter N. Vernon, "The Oddest Form of Christian Worship" in *Methodist Minutes* (Nashville: Abingdon Press, 1984), 1.

[3] Mark Galli, "Learning to Be Some Things to Some People," in *Leadership*, Fall 1991, (12:4), 37.

[4] Lyle Schaller, quoted by Galli, 37.

[5] Ibid., 37.

[6] For a detailed study of church advertising, see *Marketing the Church*, NavPress, 1988, by George Barna and *Marketing for Congregations*, Abingdon, 1992, by Norman Shawchuck, et al.

[7] See Bill Perkins, *Fatal Attractions* (Eugene, Oreg.: Harvest House Publishers, 1991), 45-118.

[8] Quoted in "Seekers or Saints: the Church's Conflict of Interest," in *Leadership*, Fall 1991, (12:4), 21-22.

[9] Galli, 20.

[10] For a more in-depth development of this concept see chapter 5, "Production Evangelism," in the authors' book *Finding Them, Keeping Them* also published by Broadman Press.

RESOURCES

Seminars:

"Heart for the Harvest" available from Search Ministries, 101 W. Ridgely Rd., Suite 5-A, Lutherville, MD 21093; (301)252-1246.

Finding Them, Keeping Them, available through the Church Growth Network, 3630 Camellia Dr., San Bernardino, CA 92404; (909) 882-5386.

"Team Evangelism" available through Church Growth Institute,

P.O. Box 4404, Lynchburg, VA 24502; (800) 553-4769

Institute of Evangelism, Billy Graham Center, Wheaton College, Wheaton, IL 60187; (708) 752-5916.

Materials:

ACTS International, P.O. Box 157, Claremont, CA 91711

"Living Proof" Small Group Video Series

Christian Business Men's Committee of USA (615) 698-4444 and NavPress (800)366-7788

"You Can Tell It," EvanTell, Inc., 1984, 92212 Markville, Dallas, TX 75243

Newsletters:

Common Ground available from Search Ministries, 101 W. Ridgely Rd.,

Suite 5-A, Lutherville, MD 21093; (301)252-1246.

For Further Reading:

Aldrich, Joseph. *Lifestyle Evangelism.* Portland, Oreg.: Multnomah Press, 1981.

Aldrich, Joseph. *Gentle Persuasion.* Portland, Oreg.: Multnomah Press, 1981.

McIntosh, Gary and Martin, Glen S. *Finding Them, Keeping Them: Ten Strategies for Evangelism and Assimilation in the Local Church.* Nashville: Broadman Press, 1991.

Peterson, Jim. *Living Proof.* Colorado Springs: Navpress, 1989.

8

*My attitude has always been: If it's worth playing,
it's worth paying the price to win.*
> —Paul "Bear" Bryant

*If you want to win in the 21st century,
you have to play the service game and play it very well.*
> —AT&T Advertising Slogan[1]

ASSIMILATION

An amusing example of technology gone bad is seen through this hypothetical voice mail received when a caller dialed 911.

> Thank you for calling 911. In order to serve you better, your call is being routed to the police department, fire department, hospital, or mortuary best able to help you.
>
> If your home is being broken into, press 1. If the intruder is armed, press 2. If the intruder is in the room from which you are making this call, press 4. If you are attempting to avoid detection and have turned off the lights, press 2339200976, followed by the pound sign.
>
> I'm sorry, that is not a valid number. Please try again.
>
> If you have been attacked since your last choice, are dazed and unable to recall long strings of random numbers, press 1. If you are bleeding, press 4. If you are bleeding all over the rug, press 5. If you would like the number of a good cleaner, press 7. If you want more options, press 1776-star, in honor of the choices opened up to humanity by the American Revolution.

If you want to know the choices in other states, press 1776 followed by the number of stars indicating the order in which that state was admitted into the union. For a listing of the order of admission, press 4. To repeat this message, press 2. If you are still bleeding, press down hard on the wound.

You're probably thinking, *It can't be that difficult to get help when you need it.* And you are correct. But more often than not, newcomers feel like they face the same kinds of obstacles when trying to find acceptance in a church.

Churches across the United States have determined that "people flow"[2] is a primary concern in programming, especially in the area of assimilation. Effective churches which are reaching their community for Jesus Christ *and* helping people assimilate into the body make people flow a priority.

Assimilation

That was then...	This is now...
▲ Visitors	▲ Guests
▲ Reserved parking for staff	▲ Reserved parking for guests
▲ Home visits	▲ Phone visits
▲ Visitors introduced	▲ Guests anonymous
▲ Responsibility is with visitor	▲ Responsibility is with church
▲ Happens by accident	▲ Happens by plan
▲ Lecture-styled facilities	▲ Relational-styled facilities
▲ Membership class	▲ Membership process
▲ Information packets	▲ Video on the church
▲ No funds	▲ Budgeted item
▲ Ushers solicited	▲ Ushers trained
▲ Back rows for members	▲ Back rows for guests
▲ "Open your Bibles"	▲ "Take out your study guides"
▲ Find friends after the service	▲ Find a guest after the service
▲ Random follow-up	▲ Organized tracking
▲ Assimilation by staff	▲ Assimilation team

Assimilation Trends

Every church falls into one of three categories.

Category 1: Hospital Churches. These are the churches which seek only to care for their own. Their programs and methods focus solely upon the felt needs of the flock and thus have an inward orientation.

Category 2: Army Churches. These churches resemble an army on the march. They have people to be won to Christ, battles to be fought, and ground to gain back from the devil.

Category 3: Mash Unit Churches. These churches combine both aspects of an army and a hospital. They are on the march, while simultaneously caring for the wounded and helping in their recovery so they can once again get into the battle.

These Mash Unit Churches are using some of the following strategies to assimilate newcomers into their body.

1. Up-to-Date Membership Class

Membership classes are nothing new. However, increasing numbers of churches are setting higher standards for membership. By placing greater expectations upon the prospective member, churches not only educate newer people about their vision, but they also challenge them to greater commitment in the church.

Several factors help membership classes be effective.

First, they are offered in a seminar format rather than a classroom format. Tables are provided for the people to take notes as the instructor teaches using an overhead projector. Refreshments are provided at the appropriate breaks, all giving the feel that the people are in a seminar.

Second, people share their testimony during the class. Various leaders and members discuss their "door of entry" into membership in the church. The time ends with a question-and-answer segment where the newcomer asks questions, practical, doctrinal, or otherwise.

Third, the vision of the church is clearly outlined. For people to stay for a short time in a church, they will need three things— friends, a ministry, and a small group.[3] But to keep people for the long haul, they must be able to identify with the direction and vision of the church. The membership class is the ideal setting to share these kinds of things with the newcomers.

2. Pastor of Assimilation

Staffing a church for growth requires a different philosophy of hiring staff than that normally employed by churches. History has shown that most churches hire a youth pastor as the second staff person, on the theory that building a youth ministry will attract adults. While a solid youth ministry is a crucial element of a growing church (see chap. 10), in a majority of cases a youth pastor should not be the second staff person called to a church.

Some growing churches are adding pastors of assimilation in an effort to keep as many newcomers as possible. The average church keeps about 16 percent of its guests, but churches employing pastors of assimilation often keep as high as 30 percent of their newcomers.

The ministry description of a pastor of assimilation includes many of the following responsibilities:

▲ recruiting, training, and overseeing greeters, parking attendants, and ushers.

▲ designing an effective follow-up process for first-, second-, and third-time guests.

▲ developing and teaching a new member class.

▲ coordinating a refreshment table for newcomers.

▲ organizing a welcome center.

3. Phone Visits

The use of the phone has changed immensely in the past ten years. In the thirty years since the first communications satellite, Telstar I, was launched, we have seen the advancement of microelectronics, microprocessing, photonics (light wave devices and systems), and optical fibers. Cellular phones are used by more than three million people in the United States, and there are more than five million radio paging units in place. And today, facsimile machines are commonplace.

The impact of this technology has been introduced into the church as well. In 1955 many churches began broadcasting recorded prayers continuously over the telephone. By the late fifties, churches across the United States were offering "dial-a-prayer" services. New York's Fifth Avenue Presbyterian Church still uses this program and averages over five hundred calls a day.

Churches now fax their Sunday School order to a company across the country. Church secretaries correspond to pastors via cellular phones. You can even order your staff luncheons by fax from the local deli. And what about that portable, wireless phone that is the size of last year's pocket calculator? You don't have one yet?

Telemarketing has become a predominant means of planting new churches and reaching out to the unchurched.[4] Home visitation is declining due to increased neighborhood crime, commuting, and the saturation of contacts experienced in everyday life.

In response, many churches use the telephone as a means of pastoral care. Phone calls have about the same appeal as a personal visit. A phone call offers the contact, the encouragement, and the impact of a visit, while respecting people's personal time.

Churches are using personal phone calls to follow up on guests and perform basic pastoral care. The coming years will see continued development of ministry by telephone. Just as pizzas are delivered, food will be provided door-to-door, videos will be rented at our driveway, and pastoral care will take place by phone.

4. Detailed Tracking of Newcomers

In every church, people are coming and going all the time. A pastor located in a major city once remarked, "It's like preaching to a parade." That being true, a system for tracking newcomers is helpful to keep up on people flow.

We will introduce a system for assimilating people into a church later in this chapter. Let us for now simply say that growing churches offer a program to follow up and follow through on new attenders. Phone calls are made, welcome letters are sent, membership classes are taught, and new people join the church. People are recruited into entry point ministries to provide a way of expressing their gifts. Small groups are started to assist people in developing friendships and the purpose, vision, and values of the church are communicated.

5. Visitor's Privacy Respected

Most of us can likely remember a time when it was expected that visitors would be publicly welcomed to a worship service. Newcomers were often asked to stand and give their name and introduce the members of their family. Some churches attached ribbons or flowers or a name tag to any visitor as a means of helping regular attenders recognize and welcome the newcomer. In days when relationships were strong and people tended to have a neighborly friendliness, this public approach to welcoming visitors worked well.

However, times have changed. We live today in an era of broken friendships, fractured families, and disconnected networks. The pressure of our informational age causes people to seek the privacy of their homes and cars, as well as protecting their personal anonymity. While visitors to a church want to be recognized, they do not want to be embarrassed by speaking publicly or being singled out with the placing of a ribbon on their clothing. Effective churches welcome their guests without embarrassing them.

6. Up-to-Date Facilities

Walk into many churches today and you will discover carpet, paint, and furnishings which look like they are from the 1950s. The interior and exterior decor of church facilities communicates much to visitors. Visitors make many judgments about a church while they are driving up to the church building and within thirty seconds after entering the doors.

Wise churches take a cue from national department and grocery chains. These stores know that times change and they must present an up-to-date image or risk being thought of as out-of-date. That is why these national chains remodel their stores on a regular time schedule. Remodeling every five years is a normal rule of thumb.

In contrast to this are churches which remodel, repaint, or recarpet their facilities only once every ten to twenty years. Is it any wonder that younger guests feel the church is out of touch with their needs? Growing churches maintain a regular remodeling schedule to keep their facilities looking great by using up-to-date colors, new carpet, and new furnishings.

7. Culturally Relevant Follow-up Plan

Follow up of first-time visitors always has been a strong point for churches. Home visitation fit the culture of a more neighborly time, and people expected and wanted a visit from the pastor.

With the rise of crime, the crowding of cities, and the desire for privacy, however, home visitation is not as culturally relevant a way to follow up visitors. Churches find it better to focus on second and third time visitors through a series of less confrontive contacts. Letters, phone calls, personal invitations to the pastor's home, and special dinners for guests at the church building have taken the place of home visitation. "Let's do lunch" not only fits the business scene but also the church scene as many guests would rather meet the pastor for lunch or breakfast. This is particularly true in communities where people are used to meetings over lunch. Of course, home visitation continues to work in some communities, but in general it does not fit our information age culture quite as well as it once did.

Increasing Assimilation in Changing Times

Church leaders understand that effective follow-up of guests is an important ingredient to their church's growth mix. Traditionally, churches have approached the assimilation of visitors simplistically with a personal visit to the home by the pastor or visitation team. Today many churches find that this method of assimilation is no longer as effective as it used to be.

1. Organize an Assimilation Process

No one assimilation strategy works in every church, but specific ingredients work more effectively than others. The process we would like to share is not new; in fact, we have seen variations in Chicago, Houston, California, and all places between.

Pastor Rick Warren has taken this to a new level at Saddleback Community Church in California. In using this format his church now provides ministry to over six thousand people in worship services. What we propose is a process that we have found to be successful.

Imagine church as a baseball field.[5] On the field are all the "players" who know the rules and how to play. They know the songs and when the offering will be taken. They know how to "play" church. In the "on-deck" circle stand the newcomers. Their desire is to play and become a part of the team, but they are a little intimidated by the game and perhaps doubt their ability.

The preaching pastor is on the mound. He has three options as they get up to bat. He can throw them a "fast ball" sermon: "Open your Bibles to the Book of Leviticus. Today, we are going to discuss the propitiating work of the sacrificial system under the dispensation of the law." He can also choose to throw them a curve ball: "Open your Bibles to 1 John which says, 'God is love.' Close your Bibles. Let's talk about the economy and the mess we are in." These two pitches (messages) either confuse or overwhelm the newcomer. Last, the pastor can throw them a "slow-pitch" sermon: "Take out your study guide and fill it in as we talk about How to Develop Loving Relationships." In other words, the slow-pitch sermon allows the newcomers to hit the ball. The idea is to help the guest get to first base so that they can "get in the game" and begin the process of becoming assimilated into the church.

The first baseline in the assimilation process teaches the newcomer how to belong.

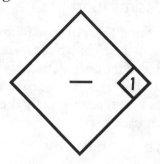

How to Belong

Here the newcomer is helped to learn the A. B. Cs.

Accept Jesus Christ as Savior.

Be baptized.

Commit to this church family.

Not every person wants to join or become a member, but everyone wants to feel a part of the group and know that they belong. So a class is designed to provide instruction for the newcomer on how to sense this oneness within the church. This class can also run in conjunction with a new believers' class which provides the basic instruction and understanding on what the Christian life is all about.

The assimilation process does not stop at first base. Few games will ever be won from there. Thus the newcomer is challenged to round first base and keep going to second base by learning how to grow.

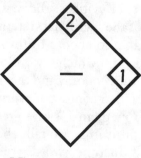

How to Grow

The design of this class is to motivate people to learn the basic ingredients that bring about maturity in their lives. At second base newcomers learn how to become F.I.T. for the Lord. After all, in order to grow, we'll need to be in shape.

Faithfulness in the Word and prayer.

Involved in giving.

Tied to a group.

So, if a person makes it to second base, they have an active devotional life, have learned the importance of giving as a spiritual discipline, and are active in a small group, recognizing that this will be the environment for mutual accountability and continued growth.

The next step is to keep them running to third base where they can learn how to serve.

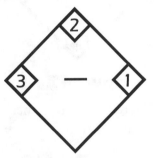

How to Serve

This class focuses on the uniqueness of the individual and God's desire for people to give their lives away in and through service. It is therefore our desire to have everyone dig into ministry. And they will do that by using their S.P.A.D.E.

Spiritual gift

Personality type

Abilities

Delights

Experiences

By developing an understanding of these five areas and identifying their giftedness, newcomers will much more likely dig into a ministry. Typically we recruit people to fill positions in the church in two ways. The first is the institutional approach. "We have a need . . . who will fill it? Any volunteers?" Here the positions may be filled, but few really own their position and have a deep sense of God's calling on their life. The second is the relational approach, which is more effective. People discover their abilities and talents, and, through a time of interview with a ministry guide, are introduced to ministries that are a match for them. Designated people are trained to teach and enable newcomers to find ministry positions that are right for them.

Obviously, no baseball games are won if the runner stays at third base, and this is true for assimilation also. Thus, to get people to home plate, we must motivate them to learn how to tell.

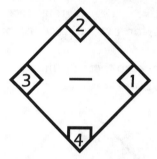

How to Tell

People learn how to tell by sharing their L.I.F.E.

Love for God and others

Invitation to church

Faith in Jesus Christ

Experience of God

Each of these baseline classes are designed to move people from the front door to the very heart of the church. They each must be manned with personnel who are enthusiastic, competent, and can articulate the vision of the church.

2. Enhance Your Friendliness

Growing churches generate a friendly environment. To create this kind of atmosphere, the attention and focus must shift from the long-term attender to the newcomer visiting your worship services. To accomplish this, try applying the following four principles.

The principle of inclusion. On any given Sunday you will have four kinds of visitors. You will have (1) Positive Transfers—those who have recently moved into your area and want to find a good church; (2) Negative Transfers—those who have become disillusioned with their own church and want a change; (3) The Saved Unchurched—those who no longer regularly attend church for one reason or another; and (4) The Unsaved Unchurched—those who have no relationship with Jesus Christ but may be searching.

Which of these groups is your primary target? How will each group view your church differently? What are their major concerns as they seek to assimilate into your church? Evaluate the practical issues of the church. Do we have enough parking? Is the seating adequate for a 10 percent increase in attendance on any given Sunday? Are visitors included in the goals of the congregation?

The principle of interpretation. Seek to understand the visitors, their world, their dreams. Do not be afraid to use your imagination. Identify those ministries in your church that may have lost effectiveness. Step into your visitors' shoes to see through their eyes the acceptance of the people, the atmosphere when they enter the church. If it is true that most people's number one fear is the fear of strangers, then your visitors will want friends and to be in a friendly place.

The principle of appreciation. Anyone who has ever bought a house knows that appreciation is what happens when something becomes more valuable over a period of time. Depreciation is like buying a car—the moment you leave the parking lot, your car becomes less valuable and you lose money.

As a church we must grow in our appreciation of the visitor. You accomplish this by people being willing to say, "We're glad you're here." This process becomes easier when visitors are directed to an information booth where they will be assisted in finding various rooms such as the nursery. This is simply a congregation's ability to stand in the gap between non-acceptance and acceptance.

The principle of selection. Select your target. Remember, when you aim at nothing, you hit it every time. Identify visitors and program for their attendance. Select the appropriate music to draw them into the body. Choose the kinds of services and messages that will make them feel at home and sense the relevancy of the Scriptures. Use terminology that is easily understood. Sensitize yourself to future perspectives rather than purely past reflection. After all, everyone can get excited about the future, but only those who have "been around" for a while can relate to the past.

3. Hire an Assimilation Pastor

Some churches are calling associate pastors that specialize in assimilation. Their job includes responsibility for developing an overall assimilation plan including some of the following elements:

▲ follow up of all guests.

▲ tracking members' attendance at worship services.

▲ recruiting and training ushers, greeters, and parking attendants.

▲ overseeing the welcome center and refreshment table.

▲ organizing the new members' and new believers' classes.

4. Recruit a Phone Team

"Telecare" is the name given to pastoral care completed by phone. You might consider using this means of providing basic care for your people. Here are a few steps to implementation.

Step 1: Identify callers. Select key leadership to oversee the program. Choose those who like to talk on the phone. Recruit people by phone to hear how they sound. Do not overlook home-makers or shut-ins as possible callers.

Step 2: Train callers. Train in sessions of about two hours. Teach callers to understand the power of words, listening skills, and how to keep a record of the call. Have callers practice by phoning each other. Provide an outline of questions to ask or ideas to talk about.

Step 3: Find phones. Use the phones at the home of the caller,or allow callers to do their work at the church using the church phones. Install an extra line dedicated for pastoral care at church.

Step 4: Call. Contact active and inactive members, shut-ins, and teenagers, excited people and apathetic people, quiet ones and compulsive talkers—everyone.

As people continue to withdraw, the church in the nineties is going to play a vital role in overcoming the loneliness that will result. The telephone may be an instrument your church can use to "Reach Out and Touch Someone."[6]

5. Develop a Welcome Center

Visit a large shopping center and you will find an information booth where you can ask questions or receive directions. Managers of these centers know that people unfamiliar with the center need help, so they provide an easy way for people to receive help.

Establishing a welcome center shows that your church cares about its guests. Place the center in a high traffic area, and staff it with friendly people who find it easy to talk to strangers. Provide information sheets on your church. If your church has several entrances, provide small welcome centers in each traffic area.

6. Use a Hospitality Table

Prior to and immediately following the worship service are good times to show hospitality to newcomers. However, guests often find it awkward to stand around waiting for someone to talk to them before the service, and after the service they are the first ones out the door and in their cars.

The well-planned use of a hospitality table provides a way to greet visitors in a comfortable setting. When people have a cup of coffee or juice in one hand and a donut in the other, they are more relaxed and willing to talk together. Locate the hospitality table where newcomers will walk by it. Recruit friendly people to be hosts, and encourage your greeters to hang around it to meet newcomers. Occasionally change the location of the table and use different colored tablecloths so that people notice it.

7. Train Hosts and Greeters

The communication that occurs in the first four minutes often determines whether strangers will remain strangers or become better acquaintances and lifetime friends. Obviously, the first four minutes are not the only criteria, but represent the critical time and opportunity to contact the people who walk through the doors of our church. The people in the ministry of greeting are the front line representatives for that important period. In a very real way, greeters hold the key to a newcomer coming to know Jesus Christ.

Every Christian is an ambassador. Colossians 3:17 says, "And whatever you do, whether in word or deed, do it all in the name of the Lord Jesus, giving thanks to God the Father through him." Second Corinthians continues that thought with these words: "We are therefore Christ's ambassadors, as though God were making his appeal through us. We implore you on Christ's behalf: Be reconciled to God" (5:18). An ambassador is a representative with a specific task. The same could be said of the greeter.

The main goal of a greeter is to extend a warm greeting to those attending your church, especially newcomers, and to treat them as guests. There is a difference between a guest and a visitor. A guest can stay as long as he or she wants. A visitor is expected to stay for a while then move on. We are to treat newcomers as guests, helping them to enjoy themselves and feel accepted. One church in southern California identified these seven objectives for their greeters:

Generate a comfortable atmosphere.

Respect a person's anonymity.

Extend a hand of friendship.

Express your genuine interest.

Treat others as the Lord would.

Encourage them to come back.

Request to meet their needs.

In addition, three basics should be encouraged in the ministry of the greeter. First, greeters should remember the names of newcomers. The better the greeter becomes in this area, the more the newcomer will feel good about the church. Second, you must learn the importance of non-verbal communication. Everyone that a greeter comes in contact with will be affected by:

▲ your handshake,

▲ your clothes,

▲ your posture,

▲ how close you stand,

▲ your smile,

▲ how you touch,

▲ the expression in your eyes,

▲ how you listen,

▲ facial expressions,

▲ your self-confidence,

▲ your appearance,

▲ your breathing,

▲ your voice tone,

▲ the way you move,

▲ your hairstyle,

▲ the way you stand.

The third need is to help newcomers get connected, by introducing them to other people. Greeters should take a lesson from the mosquito. She never waits for an opening—she makes one.

8. Track Participation

While churches are not called by God to be truant officers, they are expected to shepherd the church of God (1 Pet. 5:3), and one way to do that is to track participation. Note the simple tracking system which follows. It is designed to track people through the assimilation process suggested in #1 above. The chart below shows that Frank and Mary attended together, received a personal letter from the church, and attended the membership class (How to Belong). Mary joined the church, but Frank did not. Mary went on to take the next class available, How to Grow, designed to get her into a small group. Evidently, both joined a small group, but neither of them have plugged into a ministry yet.

The system you choose does not have to be identical to this

Name	1st	2nd	Let	HB	Mem	HG	S/G	HS	Min	HT
Mary A.	✓	✓	✓	✓		✓	✓			
Frank A.	✓	✓	✓	✓	✓		✓			

1st - Visited First Time
2nd - Visited Second Time
Let- Letter Sent
HB - How to Belong
Mem - Became a Member

HG-How to Grow
SG-Small Group Involvement
HS-How to Serve
Min-Found a Ministry
HT-How to Tell

one, but identify the process right for your community and establish the data base to accomplish the task.

Recently we visited a large church. As we stepped up to enter the front door, a lady greeted us by saying, "Hi! Is this your first visit with us?" After we replied in a positive manner, she introduced herself, asked our names, and walked with us to a welcome center. At the center she introduced us by name to the person at the desk who immediately offered help and gave us directions to important areas of the church such as rest rooms and the auditorium.

As we were about to end our conversation, an usher walked up and she introduced us to him. He then led us to our seats in the auditorium. In just a few short minutes we had been introduced to several very friendly people, had our names mentioned three times, and been given all the initial information we needed. With such a well-planned strategy, there is no wonder that this church is growing. While every church may not wish to follow this church's exact procedure, to assimilate people in today's changing times churches will need to develop a well- planned assimilation strategy.

▼

NOTES

[1] *The Pastor's Story File* (Platteville, Colo.: Saratoga Press, June 1992), 1.

[2] The term "people flow" is a church growth term referring to the flow of people in and out of a local church.

[3] *Finding Them, Keeping Them: Effective Strategies for Evangelism and Assimilation in the Local Church* (Nashville: Broadman Press, 1992).

[4] Gary McIntosh and Glen Martin, "Reach Out and Touch Someone " in *The McIntosh Church Growth Network Newsletter* (San Bernardino, Calif.: Church Growth Network, March 1991), (3:3), 2.

[5] The baseball diagram reputedly began at First Baptist Church of Modesto, Calif. The version used here is from Dr. Glen Martin's church, Community Baptist Church in Manhattan Beach, Calif.

[6] Ibid., 2.

RESOURCES

Seminars:

Finding Them, Keeping Them. Church Growth Institute, Lynchburg, VA; (800) 553-GROW.

Boomers, Busters and Assimilation. Available from the Fuller Evangelistic Institute, P.O. Box 91990, Pasadena, CA 91109-1990; (800) 999-9578.

Tapes:

George, Carl *Assimilation: Incorporating New People into the Life of Your Church;* and Robert Logan. *Assimilation: Closing the Back Door.* Both available from the Fuller Evangelistic Institute, P.O. Box 91990, Pasadena, CA 91109-1990; (800) 999-9578.

Martin, Glen S. *Keeping Them: How to Assimilate New People.* Available from the Church Growth Network, 3630 Camellia Dr., San Bernardino, CA 92404; (909) 882-5386.

McIntosh, Gary L. *Suspects or Prospects? Insights for Effective Follow-up and Assimilation of Visitors.* Available from the Church Growth Network, 3630 Camellia Dr., San Bernardino, CA 92404; (909) 882-5386.

For Further Reading:

Harre, Alan F. *Close the Back Door: Ways to Create a Caring Congregational Fellowship.* St. Louis: Concordia, 1984.

McIntosh, Gary L. and Martin, Glen S. *Finding Them, Keeping Them.* Nashville: Broadman Press, 1992.

Schaller, Lyle E. *Assimilating New Members.* Nashville: Abingdon, 1979.

Smith, Donald P. *How to Attract and Keep Active Church Members.* Louisville: Westminster/John Knox Press, 1992.

Weeks, Andrew D. *Welcome! Tools and Techniques for New Member Ministry.* Washington, D.C.: The Alban Institute, 1992.

9

*The children of the 20th century would witness more change
in their daily existence and environment
than anyone else who had ever walked the planet.*
—Paul Grey in *Time*[1]

Let the little children come to me.
—Matthew 19:14

CHILDREN'S MINISTRY

*Humpty Dumpty sat on the wall.
Humpty Dumpty had a great fall.
All the king's horses and all the king's men
Couldn't put Humpty together again.*

A familiar nursery rhyme represents a model of the world in which we live and minister. Apparently a man named Mr. Dumpty was walking down the street minding his own business. Like many of us, he faced a wall in his life and through his own strength and resources was able to overcome this obstacle and climb to the top.

Looking back, Mr. Dumpty felt satisfied and fulfilled until something distracted him. He lost his equilibrium and fell to the ground, breaking into hundreds of little pieces. Circumstances were obviously not good for Mr. Dumpty, but he tried to get help.

Mr. Dumpty turned to the government for help rather than to his neighbors or family. We know that the government got involved because Mr. Dumpty's problem was brought before the king. So moved was the king with Mr. Dumpty's needs that he called a meeting of the legislature. They dispatched all the king's consultants to analyze the situation. A "Mr. Dumpty Fix-It" law was legislated to help this poor man.

The tragedy is not what happened to Mr. Dumpty, but rather that the *best* that men could offer—harnessing all their resources, efforts, and good intentions—could not solve the problem.

This is the world in which we minister. One aspect of society has not changed—God is still the only answer. However, the way in which we reach people whose lives have been shattered has changed. Nowhere is this fact more apparent than with fractured families and broken children. Ministry must prioritize children.

Children's Ministry Trends

To realize how much ministry to children has changed, consider this comparison. Fifty years ago, the top seven problems in public schools were (1) talking, (2) chewing gum, (3) making noise, (4) running in the halls, (5) getting out of line, (6) wearing improper clothes, and (7) not putting paper in the wastebasket. Today, the top seven problems are (1) drug abuse, (2) alcohol abuse,(3) pregnancy, (4) suicide, (5) rape, (6) robbery, and (7) assault.[2]

Children's Ministry

That was then...	This is now...
▲ Cradle roll	▲ Prenatal ministry
▲ 4th-6th Sunday School	▲ Preadolescent ministry
▲ Gender-based classes	▲ Co-ed classes
▲ Children's church	▲ Children's worship
▲ Volunteer director	▲ Children's pastor
▲ Plea-based enlistment	▲ Relational enlistment
▲ Little training	▲ Ongoing training
▲ Equals baby-sitting	▲ Equals teaching and training
▲ Single teacher	▲ Team teaching
▲ Prepackaged curriculum	▲ Designed curriculum
▲ Developmental- based teaching	▲ Developmental & need-based teaching
▲ Children's classes	▲ Children's support groups

Effective ministry to today's children goes beyond a basic understanding of development issues or simple babysitting. It requires taking risks to walk alongside children weighed down with burdens of divorce, physical, emotional and sexual abuse, over-committed parents, and stress-related disorders. It requires "leadership that is informed, innovative, and passionate about seeing children come to Jesus."[3]

1. Coed Classes

In the 1950s it was common practice for Sunday School departments to be broken into boys' and girls' classes. As late as 1981 many churches continued to use this method. However, most churches began to realize that it was not the best method to have boys and girls separated. Children are not usually separated at school, on the playgrounds, or in their neighborhoods. With coed classes, boys and girls see different viewpoints on issues, learn a different perspective, and broaden their perspectives. Today, children no longer want to be with the same gender, but prefer a coed adventure in learning.

2. Pre-Adolescent Ministry

Children in fourth, fifth, and sixth grades often demonstrate a strange mixture of sophistication and childlike qualities. These "little adults" are more like the junior highers of twenty years ago than the elementary students most of us recall. Kids are growing up so much faster these days.

Exposure to adult pressures and new "heroes," such as Bart Simpson, has resulted in children who might be characterized as "elementary teenagers."

In the seventies cocaine drug use by young people under sixteen was less than 2 percent, but in the eighties it increased to over 28 percent. Marijuana use went from a low of 14 percent to a high of 27 percent.[4] In the nineties it is expected that it could go as high as 50 to 60 percent. Fifty percent of today's fifth graders and 34 percent of today's fourth graders have been pressured to try alcohol.[5] Fifteen percent of kids ten to eleven and 52 percent of those twelve to thirteen say friends have tried drugs.[6] Kids under the age of ten are the only age group in which the non-use of drugs is the norm. The good news is that these pre-teenagers are ripe for salvation. They respond to teaching about Christ and can be reached through a pre-adolescent ministry. Pre-teens are into fairness, participation, respecting authority, and desire to be accepted into a group. They must deal with peer pressure, competition, overcoming shyness, and self-esteem issues. They go through stages such as group loyalty, hero worshiping, and questioning adult modeling. A pre-adolescent ministry can handle these issues, but a fourth through sixth grade Sunday School class normally cannot. Preadolescents are the focus of entire lines of resources by many curriculum companies.

3. Children's Worship

In the middle of the twentieth century, publishing firms began offering children's church materials. Most of these offerings were simply extended Sunday School programs normally aimed for children up to sixth grade. When children reached seventh grade, they were expected to attend the adult worship, to understand it, and participate effectively in it—even though they never really experienced worship.

The new trend is to view children's church as children's worship rather than an extended Sunday School time. Geared to their levels of learning and attention spans, children's worship allows them to experience every facet of worship from preparation to benediction. Children learn to sit through a message and, yes, even enjoy it. Children in the nursery start off with two easy songs and a familiar Bible story. As the children get older, include a sermon, more music, an offering, and even ordinances of the church when "big" church is observing them.

4. Children's Pastor

The children's worker of the past usually focused on Sunday School attendance and VBS. She coordinated the nursery, pre-school, or children's church. Rarely a paid position, the children's worker was often viewed in a supportive role rather than a key player in ministry.

Today's fractured family, baby boomlet, and complex environment have created a more specialized role—the children's pastor. The children's pastor is viewed as a key player in effective ministry, often caring for children *and* their families. There is a higher level of competence and accountability. A *USA Today* poll showed just what was important to people when searching for a leader, for instance a children's pastor:

▲ 61 percent competence

▲ 15 percent ambition

▲ 6 percent intelligence

▲ 6 percent personality

▲ 6 percent ability to manipulate

▲ 4 percent good timing

▲ 2 percent familiarity.[7]

While the children's director has traditionally been a role for women, more males than ever before are shifting into the role of children's pastors.

5. Relational Recruitment

Plea-based enlistment centers around bulletin inserts/announcements, pastoral announcements from the pulpit, posters, videos showing the need, phone calls, etc., whereas relational enlistment focuses on Jesus' style. For example,

▲ Prayer: He spent all night in prayer before selection.
Luke 5:16 "slip away and pray."
Matthew 10:5–10 Instructed for service.

▲ People: He met them and built friendships.
John 1:35–39 Jesus' first converts.
Luke 4:38–39 Healing.
Luke 5:1–3 Speaking to the multitudes.

▲ Personal: His invitation was a direct and personal one. Jesus' disciples were recruited to a dream.
Matthew 4:18–19 "follow me."
Luke 5:27–28 "follow me."

▲ Practice: He did—they watched; they did—He watched.

▲ Praise: He had far more words of encouragement than rebuke.[8]

6. Prenatal Ministry

Cradle roll is still a viable program that many churches successfully implement. Since we generally think children's ministry starts at birth, we have a cradle roll. But as we head into the next century we need to meet the needs of children prior to birth. Because a child is a person at conception, we need, therefore, to minister to the child prenatally.

Prenatal ministry includes the following: setting each expectant parent up with a partner to help the couple through the pregnancy; teaching Christian-based childbirth and parenting classes; giving a tour of your church's nursery; touring your church's weekday preschool program.

7. Specialized Training

At one time the main way to train teachers was to hold a special training seminar on a Saturday morning, during church training on Sunday evening, or at monthly teachers' meetings. With the busy schedules, board meetings, school trips, and compressed family times, today there's little time for church and a lot less for teacher training. New and better approaches to teacher training are developing in churches.

Fifth Sunday training is one trend. Just what the name says, fifth Sunday training takes place on fifth Sundays four times a year. All teachers are relieved of their duties and meet together in their respective groups for training during the regular Sunday School hour. No additional time is required. As for the classes, a special speaker, video, or some other event is used in place of the usual curriculum.

Increasing Children's Ministry in Changing Times

Children's ministry is a ripe opportunity for growth in our changing times. Since 1985 the number of babies born each year has been increasing by 100,000 a year, and the birth rate exceeded that of 1950, which was a high point during the baby boom years. These children will be coming to our churches, and we need to be ready for them.[9]

1. Survey Other Churches

Many churches have already identified the need to have children's ministry as one of the primary mechanisms for reaching the unchurched. When visiting other churches, pay close attention to the design of facilities. Notice their means of advertising children's ministry to the church body. Concentrate on the curriculum they have chosen and discover why they have found this curriculum so important. Tour the rooms, nursery, and offices, jotting down ideas to use later.

2. Restructure the Training of Children's Workers

Begin by establishing a prayer group to consistently pray for the children and workers. Schedule training events at regular intervals to help the leadership anticipate their coming. Try the "fifth Sunday training" approach. Four times a year, schedule a one-to one-and-a-half-hour event to include testimonies of significant accomplishments in the children's ministry, a time for prayer, and skill development in some area of children's ministry. Resist the desire to cover too much skill development material. Most skill development will take place during the actual practice of teaching. The fifth Sunday must create vision and a clear understanding of how the children's ministry fits into the total church ministry. If possible, allow for a time of sharing their needs and concerns.

3. Target the Pre-Adolescents

The times are changing, and so is the level of sophistication of fifth and sixth grade children. This age group is fast becoming the black hole of dropouts in the church because most churches have not incorporated new ideas for reaching the pre-adolescent.

In fact, kids are growing up so fast that we no longer consider sixth graders to be children. They are now classified as adolescents. Following is an example of how today's educational system views sixth graders. The following information is taken from *The Complete Guide to Starting and Evaluating a Children's Ministry* by Herb Owen.[10]

Where do sixth-graders go to school?

1990-91 public school year as reported to the Department of Education. (Statistics gathered from 37,126 schools reporting sixth-graders enrolled.)

Schools of any grade configuration where grade 6 was the lowest grade	6,431
Schools with grades 6-8 only	5,713
Schools of any grade configuration where grade 5 was the lowest grade	1,771
Schools with grades 5-6 only	339
Schools of any grade configuration where grade 6 was the highest grade	21,815
Schools with grades K-6 only	16,599

In commenting on this chart, the author states: "These figures indicate that three times as many schools place the sixth grade as the highest grade in a school than do those who place the sixth grade as the lowest grade. Many public and private educators are recognizing that the placement of sixth graders with older children is producing negative results.

A self-contained sixth grade will, in one sense, work anywhere. But sixth-graders in middle schools face the pressure to become like the older kids (and imitate their ventures into middle-school-sin) while losing the opportunity to be leaders to the younger ones in the elementary schools."[11]

Analyze your own situation. Determine for your group when childhood ends and adolescence begins. There will not be a strong line of demarcation between the two. Elizabeth Hurlock states that puberty "must be regarded as an overlapping period, a time when the child is no longer characteristically a child because of the changes in his body and in his behavior, nor is he yet an adolescent."[12]

The following chart helps to define Hurlock's statement:[12]

Age and Puberty

1 2 3 4 5 6 7 8 9 10 11 12 13 14 15 16 17 18
Childhood   Puberty   Adolescence

The 7th is the first grade where many children enter puberty.

Wherever you draw the line, consider these four areas when contemplating a Pre-Adolescent Ministry.

Make the program fun. As the maturing fifth graders look at the junior high school and high school curriculum and emphasis, they are no longer patient about being bored for an hour in Sunday School. After all, they could be home playing Nintendo, if their parents would let them. Here are some ideas:

▲ Do something different each week. Meet outside, walk to the donut shop, find out what interests the kids and then do whatever may be feasible.

▲ Evaluate the learning environment. Is the room a children's room or a room that demonstrates the changing needs and aspirations of the pre-adolescent?

▲ Use activity as a part of the learning process. They can act out stories, play games that teach the lesson, and even sing as another way to make the program fun.

Use strong application curriculum. Most curriculum available to the fifth graders today, with the exception of a few, are into heavy Bible content. There is nothing wrong with that as long as it is brought into their world and their needs. You may be discussing the fruit of the Spirit, but realize that their questions are direct: "What's that got to do with the changes going on in my thought life and bodily functions?" Here are some ideas.

▲ Ask the kids what they would like to learn. This age is not afraid to verbalize their needs and concerns. Poll them a couple of times a year to evaluate direction and the focus of curriculum.

▲ Read about the issues that kids are facing today. The pressures that today's youth are experiencing are overwhelming. The choices are different. How can we equip these children to make the right decisions without knowing the obstacles before them?

▲ Plug the children into some form of service. Fifth graders need to catch a vision for doing something for the Lord. They can be taken to retirement homes, serve at a homeless mission, or help out in the ministries of the church.

Relate to the pre-adolescent sophistication. Flannel graphs and puppets are not going to direct their attention toward Scripture and/or the work of God in their lives. We must get the spotlight off the teacher and onto the needs of these kids who are growing all too fast. They must be a part of the discovery process not only to find God's will, but also to find themselves. Allow them several things:

▲ Responsibility to organize their classrooms.

▲ Times to brainstorm and enjoy small-group discussion.

▲ Group involvement to solve a modern-day crisis that other kids may be facing.

Make the pre-adolescent ministry part of the church's vision. Always in the top five answers to why people attend churches is the emphasis on children. A growing church strategizes how to reach their community, and a primary way is through the children. How can the children's corporate ministry be seen as a part of the church's vision?

▲ Pulpit validation and interviews

▲ Advertising

▲ Budgetary support

▲ Facility prioritizing

▲ Staffing

Kids are kids, but they are growing up a little faster than they used to. The church's responsibility is to recognize this transition and plan accordingly.

4. Hire a Children's Pastor

Much education is needed in our churches in order to establish both the vision for children's outreach and the need for a children's pastor. This is not only one of the most complex ministries in the church, but often the most overlooked despite the continual pleas for recruitment of leadership. Though probably a part-time position initially, it must be viewed as an integral part of the leadership and a vital ingredient to a holistic ministry to the family. After the initial integration has taken place, this position can begin working families and working closely with the youth pastor and youth workers to make the teamwork more cohesive.

We believe the following should describe the qualities and qualifications of any children's pastor:

▲ Led by God's Spirit at all times. This individual needs to depend upon the Lord's leading and not his or her own abilities. The person needs to seek the Lord for His leading in this ministry and follow it.

▲ The ability to lead and work well with people, possessing a humble, yet creative, capable spirit.

▲ Emotionally mature, self-controlled, and even tempered, not easily wounded by criticism.

▲ Respected by those with whom the individual will work, but especially by the senior pastor and key laity.

▲ Maturity in faith. The individual needs to know the Word well. For the larger church a minimum of a bachelors degree with a significant amount of training in children's ministry.

▲ A love of children and considerable experience in ministering to them, if only from a layperson's position.

▲ The ability to handle problems well, especially personality conflicts. This individual should not tend to run from problems, but work well under pressure, and be flexible and adjust well to sudden changes.

▲ Good health and the willingness to put in long hours without being rewarded, self-sacrificing.

▲ Self-starter who completes tasks assigned.

▲ Should have the gifts of teaching and helps, especially if the individual has the dominant gift of pastor/shepherd.

▲ Not be a gossip or have a critical spirit.

▲ If married, he or she should have a good marriage with domestic harmony.

5. Establish a Prayer Base for the Leaders

There is a tremendous amount of pressure on children and their families today. Russell Chandler wrote:

▲ 45 percent of all Americans believe that ghosts exist.

▲ 31 percent of all Americans believe that some people have magical powers.

▲ 28 percent believe in witchcraft.

▲ 24 percent believe in black magic.

▲ 20 percent believe in voodoo.

▲ 34 million Americans are concerned with inner growth, including mysticism.

▲ 43 percent of all American adults believe they have been in contact with someone who has died.

▲ 67 percent of Americans report having psychic experiences like ESP.

▲ Roughly one in four Americans believes in reincarnation.

▲ 14 percent of all Americans endorse the work of spirit mediums and trance channelers.

▲ 67 percent of adult Americans read astrology reports, and 36 percent believe they are scientific.

▲ A Northern Illinois University survey found that more than half of all Americans think extraterrestrial beings have visited the earth (a common belief in New Age circles).[13]

This is our world, and our families certainly need a prayer covering; but even more do the children's workers who are trying to reach these families.

6. Provide Visibility for the Children's Ministry

Have the pastor interview children in front of the congregation. Give monthly updates in the services to help the congregation see what they should be praying for. Create a yearly video presentation highlighting accomplishments that have taken place and the lives that have changed due to the focus and energy of this ministry. Put together a quality brochure for newcomers into the body that describes the wide variety of programs that are offered. In other words, advertise this ministry as a primary focus of the church.

7. Get the Congregation to Pray for the Children

One of the best ways to help the congregation take "ownership" for the children's ministry is for each child to be prayed for by one adult. On a three-by-five card, put down relevant information about a child and special items of interest to the child. Then give that card to a volunteer pray-er from the congregation who will be willing for a month (or quarter) to pray each week for the child.

You can have a list of generic requests for all children as well as the specific ones. If leadership approves and the pray-er so desires, the adult can periodically contact the youngster to touch base for updates and to serve as an adult friend. Such a program helps to build bridges between the generations and automatically increases adult interest in and support of the children's program. It also may increase your base of volunteers and/or workers as adults develop more of a burden for the youth of your church.

Mr. Dumpty took a great fall, but the church has the answer. It is not a "Mr. Dumpty Fix-It Law." It is the power and grace of a relationship with Jesus Christ that changes lives. And "research consistently shows that people are most likely to accept Christ as their Savior before they reach the age of eighteen. Currently, about two-thirds of all decisions for Christ happen by that age." If we estimate that 50 percent of these decisions happen while still a child, we must re-evaluate where 50 percent of all our efforts and finances go in response to this great need.

NOTES

[1] Grey, Paul, "The Astonishing 20th Century," *Time* (Special Issue Fall 1992), 27.

[2] Cunningham, Shelly, quoted in "Children's Ministry in Changing Times," in *Sundoulos* (La Mirada, Calif.: Talbot School of Theology, Summer 1992), 5.

[3] Ibid.

4 David Barton, *America: To Pray or Not to Pray* (Aledo, Tex.: Wall Builder Press, 1988), 139.

[5] "Alcohol is Leading U.S. Drug Worry," *USA Today* (January 24, 1990), 1D.

[6] *USA Today* (October 27, 1989), 1D.

[7] "Getting to the Top," *USA Today* (August 17, 1987), 1A.

[8] Brent Phillips, *Pre-Teens Scene* (Southwest Community Church, Palm Desert, Calif.).

[9] *"More Babies Than the Original Baby Boom," Inc.* (January 1992), 79.

[10] Herb Owen, *The Complete Guide to Starting and Evaluating a Children's Ministry* (Lynchburg, Va.: Church Growth Institue, 1993), 26.

[11] Ibid.

[12] Russell Chandler, *Understanding the New Age* (Waco, Tex.: Word, 1988), 20-21.

[13] George Barna, *The Frog in the Kettle* (Ventura, Calif.: Regal Books, 1990), 119.

RESOURCES

Seminars:

Children's Pastor Conference: People Church-Bakersfield, Calif.

Newsletters:

Children's Ministry Magazine. Available from Group Publishing, Box 481, Loveland, CO 80539.

Associations:

Children's Christian Ministries Association 11314 Woodley Ave. Grenada Hills, CA 91344; (818) 366-5271

For Further Reading:

Anthony, Michael, ed. *Foundations for Ministry*. Wheaton, Ill.: Victor Books, 1992. (See especially chap. 9 "The Christian Education of Children.")

Bolton, B., et. al. *Everything You Want to Know About Teaching Children Grades 1-6*. Ventura, Calif.: Regal Books, 1987.

Chamberlain, Eugene. *Today's Children*. Nashville: Convention Press, 1993. Product number 5280-29.

Elkind, David. *A Sympathetic Understanding of the Child Six to Sixteen*. Boston: Allyn and Bacon, 1971.

McMinn, Tom. *Breakthrough: Children's Sunday School Work*. Nashville: Convention Press, 1991. Product number 5163-07.

The Ministry of Childhood Education. Revised 1990. Nashville: Convention Press, 1990. Product number 5290-49.

Owen, Herb. *The Complete Guide to Starting and Evaluating a Children's Ministry*. Lynchburg, Va.: Church Growth Institute, 1993.

Richards, L. O. *Children's Ministry*. Grand Rapids, Mich.: Zondervan Publishing House, 1983.

Rochlkepartain, Jolene, ed. *Children's Ministry That Works*. Loveland, Colo.: Group Publishing, 1991.

10

Youth is such a wonderful thing,
it's a shame to waste it on the young.
—George Bernard Shaw[1]

The worst danger that confronts the younger generation
is the example set by the older generation.[2]
—Unknown

YOUTH MINISTRY

Our lives are governed by laws. They are all around us. We may not detect them regularly, but they define the world in which we live. And everyone has his favorite pet laws of life. Here are a few:

▲ Johnson's Law: There is nothing to scratch but the surface.

▲ Williams' Law: There is no mechanical problem so difficult that it cannot be solved by brute force and ignorance.

▲ Hylton's Law: No job is too small to botch.

▲ Weiler's Law: Nothing is impossible for the person who doesn't have to do it himself.[3]

Not to be outdone, let us add the Martin and McIntosh Law of Trends: If a trend is affecting society today, it probably was first detected among the youth. The past couple of decades have testified to this fact.

Yaconelli and Burns, in their book *High School Ministry*, observed: "In 1986, a general sampling of youth workers by Youth Specialties indicated that 35 to 75 percent of the adolescents in any group are not living with both of their natural families. The stable underpinning of the family is not just buckling—it has collapsed."[4]

This collapse of family has created a variety of domino-like trends. There is a growing influence of peer pressure to conform to the "in crowd." A movement to "gang" support and motivation has become an integral part of growing up for many. The fracturing of the family created a void of worthwhile heroes to model. Today's youth appear to be turning to some of the popular heroes in media and music who are often immoral, without character, and who present the impression that evil has the upper hand.

What about the trend of open sexual expression that began in the sixties? Jim Burns noted:

> In 1967, 85 percent of the teenagers surveyed believed that premarital sex was morally wrong. In 1981, only 21 percent felt it was wrong. Nearly six out of ten sixteen- to-eighteen-year-olds have had sexual intercourse. The average age for the first sexual experience is sixteen years.
>
> A conservative estimate of teenage pregnancies in a year is one million. At least a third of those pregnancies will end in abortion. Only one of every ten teenagers who get married because the woman is pregnant stays married, meaning that nine out of ten get a divorce. Teenage pregnancy is the number one cause of school dropouts for females. The suicide rate among teenage mothers is ten times that of the general population.[5]

The U.S. Children's Fund reports that every day:

▲ 16,833 women get pregnant.

▲ 2,740 of them are teenagers.

▲ 1,105 have abortions.

▲ 369 teenagers miscarry.

▲ 1,293 teenagers give birth.

▲ 6 teenagers commit suicide.

▲ 1,375 teenagers drop out of school.[6]

Obviously, many local churches have failed to reproduce the life of Christ in the life-styles of their youth in our changing times. The good news is a renewed interest in youth ministry that will carry churches into the twenty-first century. Take a look at some of the trends that are affecting youth ministries.

Youth Ministry

That was then...	This is now...
▲ Parachurch ministry	▲ Church-based ministry
▲ Evangelistic rallies	▲ Outreach events
▲ Youth workers	▲ Youth pastors
▲ On-the-job training	▲ Professional schooling
▲ Worship in the service	▲ Worship in youth meeting
▲ One youth group	▲ Groups-within-groups
▲ Unrelated events	▲ Integrated programming
▲ Told what to do	▲ Taught to think critically
▲ Focus on programs	▲ Focus on relationships
▲ Ministry to youth only	▲ Ministry to families also
▲ Fun and games	▲ Crisis intervention
▲ Centered in the suburbs	▲ Centered in the streets
▲ Simplistic	▲ Complex
▲ Disjointed program	▲ Continuity of program
▲ Led by youth pastor	▲ Led by youth teams
▲ Involves a few	▲ Involves all youth
▲ Isolates youth	▲ Links with entire church
▲ Exhausted workers	▲ Invigorated workers
▲ Youth pastor-controlled	▲ Youth pastor-empowered

Youth Ministry Trends

Creativity in youth ministry is a necessity for reaching this younger generation, as the following trends in youth ministry indicate.

1. Church-Based Ministries

During the past fifty years we have seen many parachurch youth ministries rise and then decline. Does this mean they are no longer effective? By no means! Youth for Christ USA, InterVarsity, Campus Life and similar ministries have played a substantial role in reaching youth with the gospel of Jesus Christ and have given birth to other mission organizations and youth-focused ministries. But when examining the number of field staff with these organizations, parachurch youth ministries appear to be on the decline.

An example comes from Mark Senter III who reports, "From the high of 821 during the 1979-80 school year, the organization [speaking of Youth for Christ] reported the equivalent of 549 club workers."[7] Club workers had declined 33 percent in less than ten years. Their 1987-88 study demonstrates an apparent stagnation in club enrollment, where the number of clubs in 1987-88 was approximately the same as in 1975-76.

The flip side of this decline is the rise in church-based youth ministries. Dan Spader launched the Sonlife Ministries in 1979, designed to promote the church-based evangelism and discipleship of youth. Through his ministry youth leaders and sponsors are challenged to formulate a new vision and focus for their youth strategy which reaches out to win and build disciples. Sonlife's plumbline rests upon the church's ability to create and train youth who have a "Great Commission Conscience."[8]

2. Outreach Events

By the mid-1940s, as America rebounded from the devastating impact of the depression and World War II, youth ministry had become a predominant player on the religious landscape. *Newsweek* reported the success of the Youth for Christ ministries, by printing that over sixty-five thousand people attended a Memorial Day rally.[9] Youth for Christ, five years later, shared that there were as many as 1450 such rallies taking place across the country.[10] "Rally" became the term used to describe what was happening in this area of youth ministry. However, today the youth rally is seldom used. Why are youth rallies so few and far between today?

First, baby boomers became teenagers. Their desire for intimate relationships and "high-contact" interaction sparked the desire to integrate youth work into the overall church program. Church-based ministries offered weekly gatherings and support during tumultuous times.

Second, the middle class became the predominate group. As they would be the primary beneficiaries of this movement toward church-based support for youth, they began to financially support the church's emphasis.

Third, churches began to focus on leadership development. With the transformation of society into a technological age taking place right before the church's eyes, continuing education and further training were the call of the day. By the 1960s, youth ministry was being viewed not as something you were "stuck with" but something you were "called to."

Today the competition for time is much greater than in years past. The youth of today are consumer-oriented, and so the philosophy and programs of youth ministry are a crucial consideration. With the rise of MTV, shopping malls, disc players, and various high-tech attractions available to youth, churches are having to become increasingly creative. Live bands call the meeting to order (if there is such a thing), and a drama initiates the focus on the subject of the evening. The youth pastor or leader speaks for ten to fifteen minutes in words common to their culture, addressing a felt need of this generation. A time of quiet worship and reflection may follow as students are challenged to evaluate their current life-style and future.

These kinds of outreach events are held monthly, not once or twice a year. They are thus an integral part of the planning and strategy of the church. Willow Creek's "Student Impact," in South Barrington, Illinois, ministers to over a thousand high school students each week and offers a great model of this type of outreach success.[11]

3. Multiple Ethnicity

Perhaps nowhere in the United States is the complexity of multiple ethnic groups more apparent than in southern California, with at least 150 different language groups within one hundred miles of the larger Los Angeles area. While very few cities or communities can identify with that level of ethnic diversity, most of the larger communities have no doubt noticed growth in their ethnic diversity. The world has come to America. We are the mission field.

In contrast, since the 1940s youth ministries have been predominantly mono-cultural. Youth ministries that are growing in today's environment have a much broader student makeup. *Perestroika*[12] and *glasnost*[13] have opened Europe and Russia to the world and likewise to America. The Korean Church, the fastest-growing church in the world, sends missionaries to the United States because of the influence and westernization of the Korean people who are here. The growing youth network is reflecting the same openness by providing opportunities to cooperate with other ethnic groups on summer trips, outreach activities on campus, and focus on inner-city youth. Today's youth workers are not seen as isolated workers but integrated strategists.

4. Participating in Worship

The baby boomer generation challenged the norms. They began a revolution so significant that *Time* magazine reported, "The Generation That Forgot God: The Baby Boom goes back to church and church will never be the same."[14] Not satisfied with passive observation, they wanted to experience life and God first-hand. Their baby buster children (today's youth) are no different.

When the youth of today enter the church they want to sense the presence of God. The necessity for revitalization of prayer in the life of youth and their leaders is being recognized as vital to the growth of youth ministry. Acceptance of the supernatural and the failure of secular educational philosophies have created a void in the lives of the young that can only be filled with the presence of God. The prayer summits of the Pacific Northwest, which transform the lives and ministries of pastors, are a good model to revitalize and energize the lives of youth workers throughout the country.[15]

5. Women in Leadership

While even the most conservative theologians have never denied the existence and the right of women to exercise their gifts in teaching and leadership, these gifts have most often been identified with the teaching and leading of children in the church. A new era of female leadership has come to the church, and many will find expression through youth ministries. Recent graduates in some Christian training schools are nearly 50 percent female.

The needs of today's youth demand the input of gifted women who can be advocates for girls in times of crisis. The diversity of pressures and cultural expectations must cause us to see that a woman's input is not only helpful, but vital to the health and well-being of our youth groups.

6. Higher Expectations

The past ten years have been very stressful for churches. Televangelist scandals, declining giving, and a failure to change the tide of immorality in society have generated a number of criticisms directed to the church at large. One result is a higher expectation directed toward youth workers to "turn youth around." Parents expect youth workers to do more. Consider the fact that divorce rates continue at a high level. As *Fortune* magazine reported:

The United States is the world's divorce mill, and in this decade, sadly, a lot of us are going to be headed for Splitsville. During the 1990s the Bureau of the Census reckons that somewhere between four and five out of every ten marriages will break up, a slight decline from the five out of every ten that prevailed through most of the 1980s. That drop has less to do with morals than with aging.[16]

The use of drugs and alcohol is also up. George Sumpter, surveillance detective for the Los Angeles Police Department and one of the founders of D.A.R.E.,[17] reports that two-thirds of all youth experience alcohol regularly.

Sexual immorality is up. An article in a May 1993 edition of the South Bay *Daily Breeze* in southern California reported:

> Nobody wants to leave the Prom and go straight home. The parties at the hotels are where most people are going. Generally, groups of young people pool their funds to rent a room and have parties with a large group. But students say there often are opportunities for couples to be alone, and some sexual activity is expected.[18]

Parents want to know how the church will respond. The same parents who grew up arguing for freedom of choice and questioning the establishment now expect youth leaders to minister to their teenagers and the pressures awaiting them. They want results.

7. Groups-Within-Groups

In our day of bigger is better, many youth are missing the personal relationships with adults and peers which were found in the small youth groups of years past. A trend today in some youth groups is to organize groups within youth groups to help create a more personal climate which leads to spiritual growth. Clustering youth and adults together in small communities within the larger youth group context provides the opportunity to build better relationships. Adult sponsors find the small group relationship a better place to monitor each youth's growth and development and provide a natural setting for guidance.

8. Integrated Curriculum

Youth ministry in former days was essentially a series of events with little integration. The youth program was a whirlwind of activity ranging from the youth Sunday School class to the youth prayer meeting to the youth social. Each provided an element of teaching, worship, play, growth, and socializing but often with very little integration. What happened in Sunday School often had no bearing on what happened in the social activities, for example.

The new approach being developed by some youth leaders is to integrate themes into the entire youth ministry. For instance, a theme might be "Building Godly Relationships." This theme then is integrated into the entire youth ministry curriculum. The godly relationships theme is creatively woven into the Sunday School class, prayer times, discipleship groups, retreats, one-on-one relationships, sponsor training, and socials. By allowing the youth program to focus on depth more than breadth, participating youth are challenged to make their own decisions and to grow spiritually.

9. Close-to-the-Action Decisions

Decisions affecting a local church's youth ministry are normally made at the board level by people not directly involved in the day-to-day ministry. To make matters worse, many churches do not even include the youth in the decision-making process. Youth today are clearly capable of contributing to the decision process, and it is a major mistake to leave them out of the loop. Today's youth want to be consulted about decisions that will affect them.

In addition, the well-trained youth pastor in growing youth ministries carries more decision-making authority than in past years. Candid adults admit that youth ministry today is not even close to what most of us experienced in our own youth. Effective youth pastors are not just using their ministry as a stepping stone to better positions, but they are well-trained experts with skills, abilities, and the willingness to work with adolescents. They work with the youth day to day and are equipped to make the right decisions for the youth program. Growing churches delegate much of the authority to do so directly to them.

10. Player-Coaches

The term "Lone Ranger" is a good representation of what youth ministry used to be all about. Most of us who have been youth pastors remember doing it all. We taught the youth Sunday School class, counseled at camps, scheduled the activities, and transported the kids. We were hired to "work with the youth" and any attempt to broaden that ministry, such as to parents, often was met with the statement, "We're paying you to work with the kids, not us." Thankfully, things are changing and the watchword in youth ministry today is "team" ministry. Youth pastors play the role of "player-coaches" rather than Lone Rangers in our changing world. Discipling youth today takes a cooperative effort of parents, sponsors, staff, and youth leaders to influence youth.

Improving Youth Ministry in Changing Times

A maintenance of the "status quo" and an acceptance of mediocrity will not reach today's youth. Youth ministry must continue to change and grow for a generation awakening to the spiritual void in their lives. To energize your youth ministry in our changing times, use some of the following ideas.

1. Evaluate Your Youth Ministry

Be honest! How successful is your youth ministry? We are not asking how many youth attend or how many activities have been planned for the summer, but how effective the ministry has been. Success is not a record attendance. Success is not a busy calendar year. Success is not amusement of the youth. Success is ministry that changes lives and involves people on a level that eliminates burnout.

The basis for evaluating your present structure and programming must be based upon your vision and ministry philosophy. Terry Hershey, in his book *Young Adult Ministry*, identifies six ingredients that every youth program needs to have a firm foundation.[19]

The six ingredients shown in the following chart generate a tangible way of measuring both the effectiveness of your group and the readiness of the program to grow. Is the theology of the church reflected in the ministry to the youth without stifling their ability to reach their friends? Does the programming integrate the diversity of the programs' environment, or are you content to reach the ones you have already reached and now stereotype the remainder? Is there a sense of community within the group? Do the youth and sponsors get together to encourage "one another to love and good deeds"? Are the youth a part of the church or is yours merely a ministry to provide for the parents who attend the church? Is youth ministry a part of the heart, passion, and vision of the leadership?

And lastly, is there an equipping focus where the youth are motivated and trained to serve?

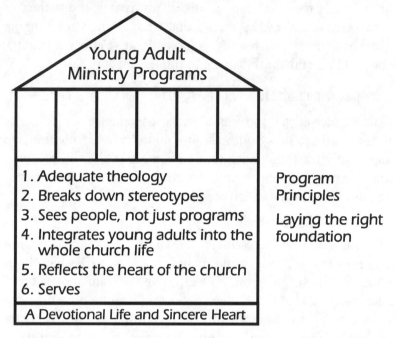

<table>
<tr><td>
1. Adequate theology
2. Breaks down stereotypes
3. Sees people, not just programs
4. Integrates young adults into the whole church life
5. Reflects the heart of the church
6. Serves
</td><td>
Program Principles

Laying the right foundation
</td></tr>
</table>

These are important questions to consider. But more than that, they should represent the beginning of all evaluation if the youth ministry is going to thrive as God would have it.

2. Provide Continuing Education

The increasing complexity of youth ministry necessitates continuing education for all youth pastors and leaders. Churches must take responsibility for providing continuing education in at least two areas.

First, continuing education provides for personal development. Leadership potential is lost when followers grow beyond your youth leader's abilities and vision. Continuing education challenges youth leaders to keep up with important trends and information. It nourishes their hearts and souls and protects them from burnout so often associated with ministry.

Second, continuing education provides for practical development. It provides for development of practical skills and motivates youth leaders to achieve. Abraham Lincoln is an excellent example of a leader who achieved much in life through continued personal development. In writing on Lincoln's leadership style, author Donald T. Phillips wrote:

> For Lincoln, the need to achieve was more than just a simple inclination; it was an uncontrollable obsession. His law partner, William Herndon, noted that he was "always calculating and planning ahead." Lincoln's ambition, wrote Herndon, "was a little engine that knew no rest." In the early years, Lincoln tried several careers in his quest to succeed in life. He ran a general store, was a postmaster, a surveyor, and eventually a lawyer and politician. His near compulsive persistence is evident over the course of his entire political career. He was a tireless worker, campaigner and public speaker.[20]

In a very practical way, Lincoln's success was tied directly to his commitment to continued education. As his personal skills increased, so did his desire to achieve.

This continued education process can be as formal as a seminary education or as informal as seminar attendance. It can also be as simple as providing the necessary funds to allow the leadership to purchase books that are on the "cutting edge" in their area of expertise. Take responsibility for the continuing education of your youth staff. Require youth leaders to attend a minimum of ten hours of training through seminars, workshops, or school programs each year. Provide a minimum of 3 percent of your youth pastor's salary to pay for this required continuing education. What this will say to your youth workers, paid and voluntary, is "you are important."

3. Share the Responsibility

No one is going to argue the fact that this generation of youth is very selfish and "me-oriented." But that could have been said about any and every generation of teenagers. The big issue today is one of priorities. Youth are being torn by the priorities of their friends, the media, their school, and the value system of their family, assuming it is still intact. Piling on guilt will not help create a greater sense of responsibility, because guilt only produces more guilt. The way to overcome an error in priorities is to provide a godly model so that youth can picture the priorities that are important. A youth pastor cannot provide this kind of caring ministry to all of the youth group. Therefore, it is important to "give away the ministry" to responsible workers and/or sponsors who can provide the care and modeling.

Give away the youth ministry to adult sponsors who will lead small groups of youth. Each adult sponsor becomes a big brother or big sister to his or her small group to provide for personal care and modeling of a godly life-style. As a personal friend to a few youth, the youth sponsor's purpose is to simply live life with the youth. Some groups may choose to play golf while others may go shopping. It becomes Deuteronomy 6:7 in action as youth see a godly life-style when "you sit in your house and when you walk by the way and when you lie down and when you rise up."

4. Provide a Balanced Program

Successful youth programs today include ministry to the youth, their families, local campuses, and a sense of continuity between the various stages of youth—namely from pre-adolescents to junior high to high school.

The great temptation that must be overcome at this point, however, is trying to imitate another church's philosophy and structure. The needs in your community and the needs of your youth are unique. Treat them as such. Make sure that your programming has these needs in mind. Determine the target audience of your ministry and aim with this target in mind. Recognize that the youth themselves must own the process and the program if they are to sell it to their friends.

Several insights should be considered when programming for your year in ministry. First, start slowly and initiate change gradually. Many youth ministries that attempt to restructure do so by overwhelming the youth, and in doing so, burn out the leadership. Second, experiment with new ministries. Remember that success does not mean that you will not fail. Failure is a part of growth and provides a wonderful arena for learning and future success. Thus, redefine failure and talking in terms of "experiments." Everyone knows that some experiments fail while others succeed. If one of your experiments fails, well, it was just an experiment after all. Third, recruit a team of youth leaders. Allow them to assume a major part in establishing the direction, maintenance and creativity of the program. This will provide a means of accountability and continual leadership development.

5. Focus on Relationships

Wayne Rice, editor of *Youthworker* and co-founder of Youth Specialties, said, "Programs won't attract kids, if only because the church can't compete with the world on that level. Today's kids are looking not for programs, but for relationships that work, for friends, even for adult friends who care about them and take them seriously." [21] The days are gone when youth ministry could survive purely as a program. Youth simply have too many other options today—MTV, videos, athletics, or just hanging out.

What today's youth do not have is what most of us lack—friends! Divorce, double income families, fractured networks due to a high mobility rate, and parents who are just too tired to listen create youth who are longing for real, honest relationships. This is why large youth groups are becoming groups within groups. This is why it takes a team ministry. This is why it takes more youth workers than ever before. It takes time and personnel to be able to meet with youth one-on-one or in small groups. But it is worth it in the pace of growth and discipleship which can be developed.

6. Unleash Your Creativity

Like any other ministry in the church, youth ministry gets into ruts. However, while adults may put up with life in a rut, youth will not. Unleash your creativity by listing all the events, activities, and programs currently being carried on in your youth ministry. Then ask a group of the newer kids, who have been in your youth program less than one year, to evaluate all that you are doing. If you are really willing to take a risk, draw together a core group of non-Christian youth and ask them to evaluate your ministry. In the business world these teams are called focus groups and are a super way to get an outsider's view of your ministry. We are not suggesting that you compromise your program biblically in any way, but simply that you let someone peek over your shoulder and give you their input. It will open your eyes and spark your creative juices. Or, if that sounds too risky, visit other youth groups to see what is being done. Call several youth pastors in your area and get together twice a year for creative sharing to enrich each other.

7. Broaden Your Concept of Youth

The basic categories of youth used to be the three areas of college/career, high school, and junior high. Today it is wiser to place the college/career group in the adult category and redefine your youth ministry to include high school, junior high, and pre-adolescents. The adolescents of today are not the thirteen-, fourteen-, and fifteen-year-olds, but the ten-, eleven-, and twelve-year-olds. Placing fourth, fifth, and sixth graders in the youth ministry arena may sound out of place, but these new adolescents are facing pressures that were reserved for the early teen years in the past.

Remember how the junior high years were the time when teenagers would drop out of church? Today, many churches are finding that the major period of drop-out has been pushed down to the fourth, fifth, and sixth grade years.

8. Redefine the Youth Pastor's Role

Today's youth pastor must be a skilled family pastor. The complexity of each student's home environment is often the cause of the problem visibly seen in each youth. Blended families, single-parent families, co-dependency situations, physical, mental, sexual, and substance abuse all must be understood by the youth pastor to be able to minister effectively to the youthful participants at church. The days of "we hired you to work only with the youth" are over. Take steps to redefine the youth pastor's role into that of a family pastor who ministers to the youth's entire family.

9. Build Parafamily Structures

Youth need the support of a family. Unfortunately, due to the high rate of divorce, many youth are growing up without the support of a traditional family unit. The rise of gangs is one way that some youth develop a substitute family, while for others it is found in sports teams or other special interest groups. Without the traditional network of parents, cousins, uncles and aunts, sisters and brothers, youth find it difficult to learn the necessary skills to function in the world. Most adults learn how to make decisions, handle conflict, negotiate, solve problems, think critically, be responsible, and how to be self-controlled within a family structure. Anyone working with youth today will notice that the loss of the traditional family structure has resulted in youth who do not have some of these life skills. Youth ministry, therefore, must focus not only on religious training but on helping many youth develop basic life skills.

Developing what are being called "parafamilies" is one way to provide for this need. Youth pastors and other adult sponsors have been sort of parafamilies for youth all along. The difference is that now there are more youth who need this additional parenting— quite frankly, more than most youth pastors and adult sponsors can handle. The answer is to develop small groups where learning can take place in a group versus one-on-one. Jesus modeled such a parafamily group as He traveled with His twelve disciples. The fact is youth become more loving, successful, and better thinkers in small-group situations. [22] Effective youth ministries in the coming years will structure around family-like groups which provide for learning and growth in a parafamily setting.

The adults of the twenty-first century are today's youth. Their values are being shaped by mothers who work outside the home, neighbors who speak a different language, and teachers who preach about the environment. They will live in a world quite different from ours. As researcher George Barna notes, "The changing nature of our society has pushed us past the point of simply being able to mark time."[23] If we are to have quality adult leaders tomorrow, we must have effective youth ministries today.

▼

NOTES

[1] Michael P. Green, *Illustrations for Biblical Preaching* (Grand Rapids, Mich.: Baker, 1989), 408.

[2] E.C. McKenzie, *Quips and Quotes* (Grand Rapids, Mich.: Baker, 1980), 575.

[3] John Peer, *1001 Logical Laws* as quoted in *Parables*, Michael Hodgin, ed. (Platteville, Colo.: Saratoga Press, May 1993), 6.

[4] Mike Yaconelli and Jim Burns, *High School Ministry* (Grand Rapids, Mich.: Zondervan, 1986), 17.

[5] Jim Burns, *The Youth Builder* (Eugene, Oreg.: Harvest House Publishers, 1988), 33. Quoting from the Alan Guttmacher Institute.

[6] *U.S. Children's Fund*, May 1990.

[7] Mark Senter III, *The Coming Revolution in Youth Ministry* (Wheaton, Ill.: Victor Books, 1992), 21.

[8] The term "Great Commission Conscience" was coined by Dr. Win Arn, a leading contributor to the church growth movement.

[9] "Wanted: A Miracle of Good Weather and the 'Youth for Christ' Rally Got It," *Newsweek* (June 11, 1945), 84.

[10] "Youth for Christ Now Covers 1,450 Cities," *Minneapolis Star* (Feb. 12, 1949), 8.

[11] For further information write Willow Creek Community Church, 67 E. Algonquin Rd., South Barrington, IL 60010.

[12] *Perestroika* is a term used by former Soviet Premier Mikhail Gorbachev in calling for "economic restructuring."

[13] *Glasnost* is another term used by former Soviet Premier Mikhail Gorbachev in challenging the former U.S.S.R. to "openness."

[14] "The Generation That Forgot God," *Time* (April 5, 1993).

[15] Joe Aldrich, *Prayer Summits* (Portland, Oreg.: Multnomah Press, 1992).

[16] Tricia Welsh, "Divorce: Getting the Best Deal," *Fortune* (May 17, 1993), 122.

[17] D.A.R.E. stands for Drug Abuse Resistance Education. For further information write D.A.R.E., P.O. Box 2090, Los Angeles, CA, 90051-0090.

[18] James Cummings, Cox News Service, "Proms: A Magic Night of Temptation," *The Daily Breeze*, May 13, 1993, C-4.

[19] Terry Hershey, *Young Adult Ministry* (Loveland, Colo.: Group Books, 1986), 83.

[20] Donald T. Phillips, *Lincoln on Leadership* (New York: Warner Books, 1992), 108.

[21] Wayne Rice, "An Agenda for Youth Ministry in the '90s," *Youthworker*, (Spring 1990), 69.

[22] For a complete discussion of this aspect of learning see Marlene LeFever, "Learning," *Youthworker* (Fall 1991), 31-36.

[23] George Barna, *The Frog in the Kettle: What Christians Need to Know About Life in the Year 2000* (Ventura, Calif.: Regal Books, 1990), 26-27.

RESOURCES

Seminars:

Youth Specialties Ministries, 1224 Greenfield Dr., El Cajon, CA 92021; (619) 440-2333. An excellent resource for training and contemporary materials. Ask for catalog of resources.

Journal:

Youthworker: The Contemporary Journal for Youth Ministry, P.O. Box 17017, N. Hollywood, CA 91615-9937. One-year subscription for $25.95.

Newsletters:

Youth Worker Update, P.O. Box 17017, N. Hollywood, CA 91615-9937. One-year subscription for $23.95.

For Further Reading:

Benson, Warren, and Senter, Mark III, eds. *The Complete Book of Youth Ministry.* Chicago: Moody Press, 1987.

Burns, Jim. *The Youth Builder.* Eugene, Oreg.: Harvest House Publishers, 1992.

Campolo, Anthony. *Ideas for Social Action: A Handbook on Mission and Service for Christian Young People.* Grand Rapids, Mich.: Zondervan, 1983.

Carney, Glandion. *Creative Urban Youth Ministry.* Cincinnati, Ohio: Standard Publishing, 1991.

Christie, Les. *Unsung Heroes: How to Recruit and Train Volunteer Youth Workers.* Grand Rapids, Mich.: Zondervan, 1987.

Farley, Ross. *Strategy for Youth Leaders.* Homebush, New South Wales: Anzea Publishers, 1991.

First Aid for Youth Groups, a series of four curriculum books focusing on issues being faced by today's youth. Available from David C. Cook Publishers, 850 N. Grove Ave., Elgin, IL 60120; (708) 741-2400

Hyde, Kenneth E. *Religion in Childhood and Adolescence.* Birmingham, Ala.: Religious Education Press, 1990.

Ludwig, Glenn E. *Keys to Building Youth Ministry.* Nashville: Abingdon Press, 1988.

Marcum, Walt. *Sharing Groups in Youth Ministry.* Nashville: Cokesbury, 1992.

Ratcliff, Donald and Davies, James, eds. *Handbook of Youth Ministry.* Birmingham, Ala.: Religious Education Press, 1991.

Robbins, Duffy. *Youth Ministry Nuts and Bolts.* Grand Rapids, Mich.: Zondervan, 1990.

Ross, Richard. *10 Tough Issues in Youth Ministry.* Nashville: Convention Press, 1992 (1-800-458-2772).

Ross, Richard. *The Work of the Minister of Youth, Revised.* Nashville: Convention Press, 1989 (1-800-458-2772).

Ross, Richard and Hayes, Judi. *Ministry with Youth in Crisis.* Nashville: Convention Press, 1988 (1-800-458-2772).

StraightTrak: Teen Bible Studies on Current Issues. 8 volumes. Nashville: Convention Press, 1992.

Youth Ministry Update. Monthly publication; subscription only. Available by calling 1-800-458-2772.

11

Some people think the proper age for a man to start thinking of marriage is when he's old enough to realize he shouldn't.
—E.C. McKenzie[1]

Now to the unmarried and to widows I say:
it is good for them to stay unmarried, as I am.
—1 Corinthians 7:8

SINGLES' MINISTRY

At some time when you were driving, you may have had occasion to use a map, and that map was probably correct. Be glad you did not live in the first century B.C. Maps were not quite as precise as our road maps of today.

In the first century B.C. most of the world was unmapped. Travelers who reached a point unknown to mapmakers often found a drawing of a dragon. The idea was to discourage anyone from going farther; and seeing dragons, monsters, and other large beasts would cause many to say, "I think this is far enough."

A story is told of a Roman battalion commander who led his troops on a mission beyond the borders of what was on the map. He sent an urgent message back to Rome asking if he should continue to advance. The message read, "Have marched off the map. Please send new orders."

In our changing world, many church leaders feel like they have marched off the map. We are facing new territory, a new world. New orders are needed; the old orders will not do, and we are off the map, particularly in understanding singles' ministry.

The eighties and nineties have bred a unique group of people, diverse in their convictions, yet unified in their hopes and aspirations. We now have over 50 million singles in our country, essentially twice as many as ten years ago. Projections are that by the end of this decade the single population will again double.

That the media clearly understands the onslaught of singles is seen in television shows such as "Three's Company" and "Full House." The classic model—Dad on the job, Mom at home baking cookies, and 2.3 children, all submissive to their parents' demands—is a diminishing minority. Moms are now working away from home; sexual freedom is widely accepted; and divorce and remarriage are common. Dr. Lee Salk reports in his book, *Familyhood,* that "three quarters of the respondents in a survey conducted in 1989 by the Washington, D.C., research firm Mellman and Lazarus Inc., defined family as 'a group of people who love and care for each other.'"[2] What . . . no "Father Knows Best"? Whatever happened to the Cleavers? Definitions of "family" are becoming broader as people concentrate their attention on function rather than form. Clearly times have changed.

Singles' Ministry

That was then...	This is now...
▲ Singles in the church	▲ Singles' ministry
▲ Singles in small groups	▲ Small groups of singles
▲ Singles' sponsors	▲ Singles' pastor
▲ Singles in the city	▲ Singles' communities
▲ Never-married singles	▲ Single parents
▲ Young singles	▲ Middle-aged singles
▲ Singles invited to church	▲ Singles targeted by church
▲ Divorced with no support	▲ Divorce recovery groups
▲ Senior widows helped	▲ Senior citizen programs
▲ Singles ignored	▲ Singles cared for

A careful study of the Scriptures reveals God's love and concern for individuals who are single. God's vision for His church includes those who, in their singleness, whether deliberate or not, are struggling with identity and acceptance.

We forget that there are benefits to both marriage and singleness. Marie Edwards and Eleanor Hoover, in their book *The Challenge of Being Single,* gave some contrasts between the two:

Single	Married
Privacy: Being able to think and create without interruption in a peaceful atmosphere.	Companionship: Being held and loved; feeling another's presence; hearing another's voice.
Time: Having time to travel; cultivate talents; relax; entertain and be entertained.	Family: Having children and sharing in their love; having grandchildren as you grow older.
Freedom: Being able to choose; to make decisions; to form friendships; to use your time as you wish.	Help: Sharing the work; having another point of view when making decisions.
Opportunity: to extend borders of friendships; develop skills; move to new jobs and places.	Security: Having someone to look after you; having greater financial support.[3]

There are benefits to both groups. Each is unique, and each has specific needs that must be addressed. However, in these changing times, singles are becoming a larger component of our culture. If we are to reach this group, we must become aware of the growing trends and characteristics and then plan efficiently to target them.

Singles' Ministry Trends

There is a maxim in today's business world that those who plan by building on the past rather than anticipating the future are destined to fail. And this is certainly true in the arena of singles' ministry. Before we consider some ideas for singles' ministry in our changing times, let's look at some of the striking trends.

1. Divorce Recovery Groups

Fifty percent of all marriages in the nineties will end in a divorce. According to *Newsweek*, January 13, 1992:

> In 1965, the divorce rate was 2.5 per 1000 population; by 1976, it had doubled, to 5.0. Through most of the 1970s and the 1980s, a million children a year watched their parents split up. Instead of broken homes, there were "single-parent households" and "blended families"—as though sanitized titles could hide the messy reality of families torn asunder.

In 1990, 1,175,000 couples were divorced, and 1,045,000 children were involved in these divorces. Over the past 20 years, the proportion of people who marry three or more times increased from 4 percent of marriages to 8 percent of the total. Preliminary data indicate that children of divorce, particularly women, have a higher chance of getting divorced themselves than children of intact families.

Sadly, there does not seem to be much on the horizon to reverse this trend.

Divorced people come in all ages including the divorced teenager. They are from all vocations, backgrounds, incomes, and value systems. They are in our churches, trying desperately to adjust to separation and loss. Some are raising kids. All are wrestling with feelings of inadequacy and guilt.

We have identified three adjustment periods typical of all those who have been formerly married: crisis, conflict, and confidence.

Period #1: Crisis. This period of adjustment represents the first three to five months after a divorce. The newly divorced person is in such need of support that he or she will go to great lengths to find it. They run up their credit lines, overextend themselves with friendships, and attend social functions to constantly avoid the issues of blame and anger. They need . . .

▲ A listening ear from people who will not reject them when they share their hurts.

▲ A hug from others who have experienced some of the same pain and yet have overcome.

▲ Education on how to cope with these newfound feelings.

Period #2: Conflict. Times of conflict are revealed as the divorced person seeks to leave past relationships and develop new ones. Difficult questions continually nag at them, like . . .

▲ Who gets "custody" of the friends?

▲ How will I be "labeled" by other people?

▲ Is it okay to be single?

In these times of conflict these searchers need . . .

▲ Education on developing relationships.

▲ Prayer to deal with bitterness and forgiveness.

▲ Friends who are available to aid in decision making.

This second period lasts from six months to two years.

Period #3: Confidence. Approximately two years after the finalization of a divorce, emotions and stress finally settle. Inner anger subsides, and dating may become a part of life, even though there are still relational struggles to deal with. This is a time of new beginnings. People take some classes, reevaluate their living area, begin a new hobby, or simply accept the reality of singleness with confidence. But they still have needs like . . .

▲ A place to share like experiences as they try new things.

▲ Education for decision making and financial security.

▲ Friends who accept them just as they are.

2. Needs-Based Ministries

The younger generation finds great difficulty in making commitments. They have been characterized as the "Me" generation. They long for intimacy but are repelled by the self-sacrifices and responsibilities that may accompany it. Many are perennial adolescents afraid of growing up who, by choice, postpone marital obligations.

They have many needs, probably too numerous to address in this brief format, but worthy of some insights when programming for a singles' ministry to reach them.

▲ They are skeptical of "organized" religion but open to contacts and events which do not have a "churchy" feel.

▲ They fear their biological clocks. While attending weddings and/or funerals, they sense time slipping away, especially when they are alone.

▲ They are searching for ways to meet the opposite sex. Not long ago, *Cosmopolitan* magazine did a survey to identify where today's singles are meeting their dates. Their study revealed: 42 percent meet at parties and get-togethers with friends; 31 percent meet at work; 26 percent meet at singles' "hangouts"; 18 percent meet at classes or clubs; and 2 percent use personal ads or have blind dates.[4]

The church must provide attractive points of contact for these singles who are content with the narcissistic life-style.

▲ The baby-boomer is a procrastinator. So leadership must be aware of the need to follow up and be persistent.

▲ Many singles are committed to goals and careers. If the church is to be relevant to these singles, education must help with issues like time management, goal setting, career planning, and evaluating priorities.

▲ The boomer is very active. Events should include trips, retreats, and activities where fitness is emphasized.

▲ Many are lonely. To have a baby boomer in a group does not mean that they are fully assimilated. This constant struggle often rests on the weary shoulders of the leadership. These singles need attention and the most precious of commodities, your time.

All this research indicates a need to base and design the effective singles' ministry around the target audience. If the church is predominantly young singles, then there will be a need to offer a wide variety of "entry points" into the church.

3. Single-Parent Ministries

The fastest growing segment of our society today is the single mother. Her task is no easy one as she seeks to be both disciplinarian and mom, cook and "Ms. Fix-it," counselor and teacher to her kids. Add to these factors that the median income for a woman who is head of the home is just over half that of male-led households and you have a stressed-out family. Her needs?

▲ Help in fulfilling the dual responsibilities of both parents.

▲ Guidance in financial matters as 80 percent of all custody suits go to the mother, while only 40 to 50 percent receive full support.

▲ Help in supporting the children who suffer with loss and guilt.

▲ Education for disciplining the children.

The single dad has equal the pressures but is often overlooked in our society. He typically has not been the nurturing agent in the life of his children and now will be exposed to a whole new realm of emotions. Being the bread winner will be simple in comparison to being the counselor and nurturer that the average man is not nearly equipped to do. His needs?

▲ If the father wins custody, it usually is accompanied by numerous battles in the judicial system. The pain from these cases can paralyze the emotions of both the father and children, and support is crucial.

▲ Education on parenting skills and relational skills.

▲ Friends to confide in to eliminate or at least decrease stress. Time management is overwhelming as the father tries to keep up with sports schedules and school schedules and health problems. They often cannot see the forest from the trees and need assistance in planning for the future.

4. Postponed Marriage

Some "experts" have designated that the world of the middle-aged single adult begins for women after the age of twenty-six and for men after the age of thirty-two. Such a life-stage is characterized by a feeling of alienation and desperation. Social scientists are now becoming more convinced that we can get as old as forty-five to fifty before sensing the middle-ages. Whatever the age category, the church must begin to facilitate the growth through those evaluative years. Here are several specific issues to consider.

▲ This is an age of extreme change. Where change used to be invited into their lives as a friend, change now has become an enemy.

▲ These are stressful years as they become more aware of their own insecurities, new loneliness, and pending retirement.

▲ The middle agers are often inflexible because of inadequacies and fears.

▲ There will be disillusionment—professionally, personally, familially, and socially. Those ideals are all being challenged as they become increasingly aware of their own limitations and weaknesses.

▲ A realization sets in about the loss of parents, if they are still alive. Those external stabilizers or expectations are no longer available. They are on their own; holding the prior generations responsible is now futile.

▲ Death is seen as inevitable. Many live in a state of denial of the possibility of death.

▲ Many become convinced that they have missed the "good life." They become convinced that friends, family, and job no longer afford them the kind of contentment and fulfillment of years gone by. Some "bail out" on their relationships and drop out of their careers in search of a new vitality.

▲ Since the children are often gone, family life has changed. A commitment to a prior life-style is no longer possible.

▲ There will be increasing financial demands. This was not quite as obvious in earlier years; but as one grows older and physical limitations set in, times of retreat and relief are anticipated and enjoyed.

5. Targeting Younger Singles

Here we find the generation following the baby boomers, a generation growing up in families of divorce, latch key children, and limitations of all sorts. Social programs are being cut back, financial grants are getting harder to get, technical demands of the workplace increase while there is a decrease in the quality of education. This generation has fewer options, and what options are available must be calculated very carefully to determine if they will meet their needs. They are looking for faith that is real and that works, and if the church offers help that meets their needs, they will embrace it; if not, they will reject it.

Growing churches throughout the country see baby busters as a primary unreached community that, when targeted with specific ministries, will respond to the gospel and come to church.

6. Singles' Pastors

You have heard it said many times, "It will only fly if it gets pastoral support." Understanding that the call of leadership is to "equip the saints for the work of ministry" (Eph. 4:12, NKJV) is not enough. There must be staff accountability and staff support for all ministries in the church. A pastor of singles' ministry will provide three important things:

Direction. A ministry without someone steering the ship will tend to lose energy and motivation. Providing a staff liaison to this group will keep them moving in the same direction under the same vision.

Support. By hiring a singles' pastor you are saying to this audience, "You are important, and the church does care." The most precious commodity available today is that of time. A singles' pastor can offer the time needed to this ministry and provide the greatest ability of all, availability.

Expertise. Where can singles in your church turn for advice and counsel? They probably do not feel comfortable with the "family pastors" because they promote marital commitment and parental responsibility. They will not turn to the youth or children's pastor. What about the senior pastor? When they ask for help, often their hurts are so complex that the typical pastor or leader is not adept at solving their issues. A pastor devoted to the area of singles and singleness offers a listening and available ear in the difficult times.

7. Small Group Support

The March 1, 1993, issue of the *New York Times,* had an amazing article by Peter Steinfels titled "Churchgoings' Stamp on Office Ethics." In this article the writer stated:

> Churchgoers often do behave like everyone else. Although more likely than other Americans to endorse strict ethical standards in the workplace, they are still not so strict about questionable behavior that employers can replace their auditors with choirmasters.
>
> But the study did find that Americans belonging to small religious groups that meet frequently and that usually have fewer than 20 members are significantly less likely to bend the rules at work or approve of those who do.
>
> Such "religious fellowship groups" are quite widespread, said Professor Wuthnow (A sociologist of religion at Princeton University) . . . About a fifth of the American labor force claimed to be active in a group of this kind, which he said included Bible Study groups, prayer groups and some self-help or community action groups with a strong religious basis.

Small groups make a difference in the lives of the people who are in them. The single community desires the fellowship and communion of other people who are on the same spiritual pilgrimage as they are. This does not mean, however, that all singles must be in a singles' small group. Many singles find fulfillment in being with other married couples who may have encountered some of the same struggles which they are experiencing.

We shared in our book *Finding Them, Keeping Them,* that there are generally four ingredients to successful small groups: sharing, support, service, and study. Each small group can differ in priorities and time committed to each area, but all have these attributes as an integral part of the small group life. Singles are looking for a place to belong and grow without the threat of rejection.

Increasing Singles' Ministry in Changing Times

As we examine what is taking place in singles' ministry, we believe God is creating new ministries to meet this challenge. Think about the following as you seek to minister to this growing group.

1. Evaluate Your Church's Readiness

We have determined that there are six levels that can be identified in singles' ministries across the country. They each build upon the former with the right leadership and motivation. They can be pictured as a pyramid.

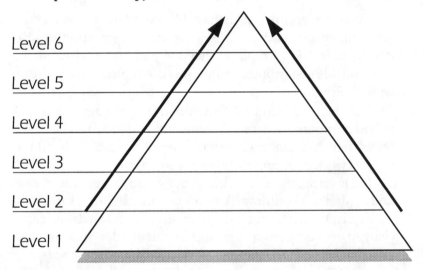

Level 6
Level 5
Level 4
Level 3
Level 2
Level 1

Level 1: Isolation. Ninety percent of all churches in the United States find themselves in level one. They have a few singles in the church who are active and participate in church functions but do not have a sense of belonging to others who are struggling with like problems and a similar life situation.

▲ Are there singles in your church who are faithful but seem lonely?

▲ Do singles in your church go to other churches for friendships and community?

▲ Is there a forum where singles' problems can be addressed and aided?

Level 2: Identification. Churches at this level have come to an awareness that they have singles in their midst but have not yet established any formal training or ministry opportunities for them. The singles are accepted and welcomed by the leadership, but simply do not fit into the overall ministry vision.

▲ Have there been any singles who seek a place of their own in your church?

▲ Have you noticed that your singles socialize in a group on their own?

▲ Are there people who recognize that the needs of their single friends are not being met?

Level 3: Instigation. These churches see the need but have no idea where to start. They may plan a small group for singles. They may host a divorce recovery seminar. They may even make several attempts at polling the church to see if there will be any response. They are hesitant, however, because there is no "staff" to oversee the ministry.

▲ Are there occasional outreach events targeting the singles' audience?

▲ Has your church identified the need to formulate and begin a singles' ministry?

▲ Are there at least a few people who have a singles' ministry vision and can get a ministry started?

Level 4: Implementation. A ministry or program begins. Usually a layperson in the church has a burden for this kind of ministry or has been deeply affected by another church's program, so they step to the front to provide leadership and stability as it gets off the ground. These layleaders will typically report to paid staff who have no technical expertise or training in singles' ministry but want to support the group.

▲ Do we have leadership in our church committed to the beginning of a singles' ministry?

▲ Does the senior pastor demonstrate the desire to see this ministry get under way?

▲ Have some of our singles been impacted by other singles' ministries and want to be a part of the leadership to get it running smoothly?

Level 5: Initiation. At this level are churches with full-time staff solely focusing their time and energies on the singles' ministry. There will be a line item in the budget designated for their use. Sadly, few churches reach this level; nationally 5 percent is considered a fair estimation.

▲ Has the church hired a full-time singles' pastor?

▲ Is there a system of continuing education in place for the development of future singles' leaders?

▲ Does the budget reflect a singles' ministry focus?

Level 6: Integration. Churches at this level consider singles' ministries as one of the primary forms of outreach into the community. Singles are targeted, and advertisement is singles-focused. There are only a few churches that are at level 6 and these are in geographical areas where the singles' movement is the strongest.

▲ Does the advertising strategy of your church demonstrate a desire to reach the singles' community?

▲ Is there continual pulpit and leadership support of the singles' ministry?

▲ Are singles an integral part of the leadership of the church?

At what level do you believe your church to be?

2. Collect Data

Traditional definitions of the term "single" have changed. There are myths that are associated with singles. So three areas must be researched and evaluated before you establish a plan.

▲ The church's perception of singles' ministries

▲ The specific age and needs of the singles in your church

▲ The number and types of singles you will choose to target

There are a number of myths that some churches have accepted. Here are just a few of the popular myths of today:

▲ All singles have no values.

▲ All singles are sexually active.

▲ All singles have very few priorities.

These and other myths must be refuted when establishing a singles' ministry that will be both effective and efficient.

In a survey of churches with and without singles' ministries, research indicated there were similarities in their reasons for not having a singles' ministry. The following were the top ten:

1. We tried this ministry before with little response.
2. Our ministry style is more "family" oriented.
3. We don't see a significant need in our community.
4. Singles' ministries are simply "meat-markets."
5. We have no single people in our church.
6. It's not in our budget.
7. Divorce is sin, and we will not condone that life-style.
8. It is not a part of the pastor's vision.
9. This ministry is too time consuming.
10. It will give the church a bad reputation.

We are convinced that these are merely smoke screens of ignorance which can be eliminated when God's people desire to reach their community by including the singles.

We suggest that leadership compile a list of every single who is ministered to through the church and then segregate the list into categories such as young single, middle aged single, single parent, separated single, etc.

Next, see if there are enough in an individual group to establish a small group. When designing a singles' ministry we have found a need to identify the "critical mass" necessary to start the ministry. It should be noted that the younger the age of the singles' group identified, the higher the numbers needed to meet the critical mass. This concept is noted in the following graph:

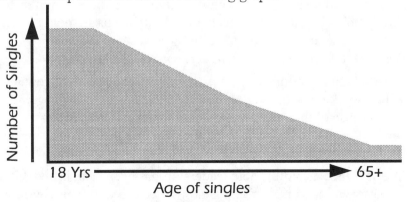

18 Yrs ————————————————→ 65+

Number of Singles

Age of singles

For example, a career singles' ministry targeting the age group of twenty to thirty years old will need a higher number than a widow support system of sixty-year-old women. The older women will enjoy being together to sit and talk about their families, write letters to missionaries, and other activities requiring less activity. The younger career singles will need a contact point with some energy. They will not be drawn to three or four people gathering for a potluck. This is the reason why there are few singles' ministries in churches with under three hundred people in morning attendance.

3. Establish a Plan

We have identified a basic plan of attack that can be molded and appropriated to every type of singles' ministry. Our approach is shown in the following figure:

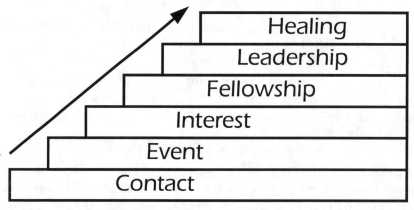

The task at hand is to take the informed insights that were previously noted and the list you have just made and make them relevant to the single in the church arena. It is never enough to simply point out an area of need. Good intentions are not enough when people are involved. One thing is certain: *No program can meet all the needs of all the singles that you have already listed.*

Contact. In targeting any group, there has to be a point of contact. When working with singles, however, there is a need for greater tact because of their fears and defense mechanisms. Through your contacts, enlist individuals to be the core of a leadership team for the future singles' ministry.

Event. Once a credible core leadership has been established with at least two individuals, there is now a need to create an environment where bonding can take place: the event level. This level involves more than just a contact and invitation; it is often the rallying point demonstrating the potential of this ministry. But remember, each group as we have already detected is unique and will want different social activities.

Here are several suggestions:

▲ Make the event non-"churchy." Don't have a heavy Bible study or extended prayer time. Visitors will be threatened by this approach.

▲ Make the event non-formal. Allow these singles to be themselves. Note: an older singles' group will typically desire a more formal setting.

▲ Make the event non-threatening. This time is for fun and bonding. Don't play anything embarrassing.

Interest. If the event was planned well, you have generated the beginnings of your singles' group. The next step toward a greater commitment will come when this interest is directed toward a time investment with other like singles.

In most churches, this has typically happened in a Sunday School setting. However, we have seen a growing trend toward singles sharing in support groups that meet during the week away from the church facilities.

Two key ingredients are vital to this level. First, the leader must be both a model and a leader. Singles seek a mentor who can help them through the difficulties and frustrations they are facing. The single mother is struggling with guilt as she is forced to work and have her children in day care for extended periods of time. The empty-nesters are wrestling with fears and loneliness as their children begin their lives of independence. The career-agers wonder how to balance a drive for success and a desire for a family. Every group has their "hot buttons."

Fellowship. This level provides a place for singles to belong. For singles to "step outside" of their comfort zone can be threatening. Trusting a new environment may mean the difference between an existence that is defensive or enriching. Within the boundaries of a small group context, a single can willingly experiment with friendships and learning. They can risk success and failure without retaliation. The group forum provides the setting where they again may have a "second chance" at a family experience.

The leaders' role in this group is not to try to take away all the individual defenses of the singles, but rather to offer new criteria by which they can reach possible recovery and maturity. The success of this level is highly dependent upon the success of the prior three levels.

Time-out. Before we move on to the last two levels of leadership and healing, it is important to recognize that the first four levels are constantly in flux. Other singles may look for a point of contact. Monthly socials can aid the group in providing events sparking interest in this ministry. Do not stop working on the beginnings of the cycle while focusing on the culmination of the cycle. There must be a consistent flow and openness to new friendships and people searching for exactly what the ministry is offering.

It has been our experience that it will take about eight to twelve months of deliberate prayer, encouragement, and support before anyone will be ready for the leadership level. There will be drop-outs. Such commitment cannot be forced.

Leadership. If there is any one cause for short-term success with no long-term lifespan of a ministry, it is the failure to generate leadership. This level is vital! In the process of several months together, you will be able to identify those who can lead and care for others. It may not be obvious at first, but we have always seen leaders emerge when given the freedom. These leaders will need considerable prime-time energy and commitment from you as the "designated" leader. You should begin to meet separately with this leadership core, once a month, for evaluation and planning of the group's life. This group is not to be considered their "fellowship" group. This is a level beyond where skill-development occurs and a challenge to help others get to this level is accepted.

Leadership development will be a continual need. A well-thought-out singles' program has processed through many key areas of leadership. First, a thriving singles' ministry has a well-defined vision statement. This vision is ever before the troops as a motivation and encouragement. Second, training is provided. The church must become a resource center for skill development of its leadership. Read books, watch videos, or visit other churches with successful singles' programs. Third, focus on building a team. Seek the further commitment to stay with the program for the long haul—until they accomplish their objectives.

Healing. For some groups the last level will be the result of your extensive involvement. After possibly ten to twelve months of involvement, blood, sweat, and tears, one of your core leaders steps out in faith desiring to lead a group of his own. These singles will warrant little attention and yet demand the greatest skill in leadership; they should not be a "hobby" of the well-intentioned pastor who is trying something new.

The bottom line issue for those who enter this level of activity and maturity is that they have worked through their own behavioral complexes and now desire to undertake the development of group life without any professional guidance.

4. Integrate Singles into Every Area of the Church

In order to remove the "blind spots" in many of the areas of ministry in your church, the leadership must be in touch with those ministries. A large church in the Midwest had been struggling with losing young families for several years. They decided to interview several of the young couples who no longer attended their church, and what they discovered was a shock to the leadership. Most of the couples interviewed loved the church and its ministry. Most of them wished they could stay. Then why had they moved on? The main reason was the look of the nursery. The wallpaper was peeling in several spots; it needed a paint job; the toys were old; and the overall appearance was not inviting. The average age of the leadership was well into their fifties. A leadership out of touch will miss their target audience every time.

Likewise, if the single community is not included in the overall planning and vision of the leadership in the church, they may be overlooked. How many singles are in the leadership of your church? How many singles are aiding in the choosing of curriculum in your church? What input do the singles have in advertising, programming, and outreach? These are all important questions vital to the integration of singles within the body.

5. Prioritize the Assimilation of Singles

This will be no easy task due to the diversity of the people involved. Here are five principles which we would offer to those accepting this challenge.

Begin the process with education. For any plan to succeed, education must be part of the process. Share your dream with key leaders and open their eyes to the need.

Commit a full year to getting started. Things may initially move slowly as the church and its leadership may never have had this priority or vision. Do not get discouraged. Review, adapt, and meet regularly to evaluate the progress.

Poll all newcomers. One of the most difficult things to do in any ministry is to adjust to change and need demands. By meeting or calling all newcomers you will quickly identify your program's weaknesses and developmental needs.

Make small groups a priority. There is no better place for assimilation than a small-group setting which provides a non-threatening environment where the initial bonding can take place.

Offer quarterly retreats. Singles need a sense of identity. This may mean that the ministry occasionally meets away from the church at a nearby restaurant, hotel meeting room, or retreat center. Initially this kind of community environment is much more comfortable to many people, but it can easily be incorporated back into the church structure when unity and oneness happens in the group.

When he was eighty-eight, the late Supreme Court Justice Oliver Wendell Holmes found himself on a train. The conductor called for tickets, but Justice Holmes couldn't find his and seemed terribly upset. He searched his pockets and fumbled through his wallet without success. The conductor was sympathetic. "Don't worry, Mr. Holmes," he said. "The Pennsylvania Railroad will be happy to trust you. When you reach your destination you'll probably find the ticket and you can mail it to us." The conductor's kindness did not put Holmes at ease. He said, "My dear man, my problem is not *'Where is my ticket?'* It is *'Where am I going?'*"

Most churches experience a similar problem. The resources may be available—they are sold on the *ticket,*—but they fail to know where they are going. Ministry to singles in changing times necessitates a re-evaluation of the church's priorities and a commitment to include them.

▼

NOTES

[1] *Quips and Quotes* (Grand Rapids, Mich.: Baker, 1980), 320.

[2] Lee Salk, *Familyhood* (New York: Simon and Schuster, 1992), 23.

[3] Marie Edwards and Eleanor Hoover, *The Challenge of Being Single* (Canada: Prentice Hall, 1974).

[4] Claudia Bowen, "What Are Men Really Like Today: Survey Results" *Cosmopolitan* (May 1986), 263–268.

RESOURCES

Seminars:

Singles' Ministry Resources Leadership Training Group, P.O. Box 60430, Colorado Springs, CO 80960-0430 (719) 635-6020.

Video:

Smith, Dr. Harold Ivan. *One Is a Whole Number.* Gospel Films, 1985.

Newsletters:

Single Adult Ministries Journal, P.O. Box 60430, Colorado Springs, CO 80960-0430.

Christian Single Magazine, 127 Ninth Ave. North, Nashville, TN 37234.

For Further Reading:

Arnold, William and Fohl, Margaret. *When You Are Alone.* Philadelphia: Westminster Press, 1990.

Barnes, Robert G. Jr. *Single Parenting—A Wilderness Journey.* Wheaton, Ill.: Tyndale House Publishers, 1988.

Bustanoby, Andre. *But I Didn't Want a Divorce.* Grand Rapids, Mich.: Zondervan, 1978.

Cavanaugh, Michael P. and McCarthy, Susan M. *God's Call to the Single Adult: A Study Guide.* Lima, NY: Elim Fellowship, 1988.

Chapman, Gary. *Hope for the Separated.* Chicago: Moody Press, 1982.

Duin, Julia. *Wholly Single.* Wheaton, Ill.: Harold Shaw Publishers, 1991.

Martin, Glen S. *Single, But Not Alone.* Church Growth Institute, P.O. Box 4404, Lynchburg, Va. 24502 (1993)

Martin, Dr. Glen S. The Complete Guide to Starting and Evaluating a Single's Ministry. Church Growth Institute, P.O. Box 4404, Lynchburg, Va. 24502 (1993)

McDowell, Josh. *Secret of Loving: How a Lasting Intimate Relationship Can Be Yours.* San Bernardino, Calif.: Here's Life Publishers, 1985.

Menconi, Peace, and Coleman. *Transitions—Savoring the Seasons of Life.* Colorado Springs: NavPress, 1988.

Morgan, Richard L. *Is There Life After Divorce in the Church?* Atlanta: John Knox Press/Westminster, 1975.

Reed, Bobbie. *Single on Sunday: A Manual for Successful Single Adult Ministries.* St. Louis, Mo.: Concordia Publishing House, 1979.

Smith, Joanne & Biggs, Judy. *How to Say Goodbye: Working Through Personal Grief.* Lynnwood, Wa.: Aglow Publications, 1990.

Sparks, Doug. *Hope for the Hurting.* Colorado Springs: NavPress, 1990.

Streeter, Carole Sanderson. *Reflections for Women Alone.* Wheaton, Ill.: Victor Books, 1987.

Thompson, Mervin E. *Starting Over Single.* Burnsville, Minn.: Prince of Peace, 1985.

Witte, Karen. *Great Leaps in a Single Bound.* Minneapolis: Bethany House Publishers, 1982.

Education:

In conjunction with the Network of Single Adult Leaders (NSL), Northern Baptist Theological Seminary of Chicago now offers a D.Min. in Single Adult Ministry. For information, contact Robert Duffet, Director of Doctoral Studies, Northern Baptist Theological Seminary, 660 East Butterfield Road, Lombard, IL 60148-5698; (708) 620-2108.

12

Nobody made a greater mistake
than he who did nothing because he could only do a little.
　—Edmund Burke

Foolish consistency
is the hobgoblin of little minds.
　—Ralph Waldo Emerson

CHRISTIAN EDUCATION

What is the most difficult ministry in a church to change? That which has been successful before. As Dr. Haddon Robinson says, "the hardest thing to change is what has worked before."[1]

To President Jackson:

The canal system of this country is being threatened by the spread of a new form of transportation known as "railroads." The federal government must preserve the canals for the following reasons:

1. If the canal boats are supplanted by railroads, serious unemployment will result. Captains, cooks, drivers, hostlers, repairmen and lock tenders will be left without means of livelihood, not to mention the numerous farmers now employed in growing hay for horses.

2. Boat builders would suffer. Towline, whip, and harness makers would be left destitute.

3. Canal boats are absolutely essential to the defense of the United States. In the event of the expected trouble with En-

gland, the Erie Canal would be the only means by which we could ever move the supplies so vital to modern war.

As you may well know, Mr. President, the "railroad carriages" are pulled at the enormous speed of fifteen miles per hour by "engines" which endanger the life and limb of passengers, roar and snort their way through the countryside, setting fire to crops, scaring the livestock and frightening women and children. The Almighty never intended that people should travel at such breakneck speed.

Martin Van Buren
Governor of New York
January 31, 1829[2]

One of the success stories of the church in the United States has been in Christian education, particularly Sunday School. Not many stories of evangelism, discipleship, and training can match that of Christian education over the past two hundred years of ministry. Yet, it is precisely due to its great success that the Christian education ministries of many churches are floundering in our changing times. The success of the past is lulling many in education to sleep as they continue to do things that worked in the past but are not as effective today.

Christian Education Ministry Trends

Buggy whip makers of the late 1800s must have wondered what to do. Noisy contraptions called automobiles were belching down streets, frightening horses and threatening to take away their livelihood. They must have realized that with improvements, these new inventions would provide faster and more comfortable travel. They must have realized that they were seeing history in the making. They must have been unsure how to adapt to their changing times.

Some of us, perhaps many of us, living today have a kindred spirit stretching back nearly one hundred years to those buggy whip makers. We see life changing and realize we must adapt. Here are some changes taking place in Christian education and some ideas on how to adapt.

1. Stress Application

It is no surprise that Christian education's primary focus was on teaching Bible "content." Promises such as "So shall my word be which goes forth from My mouth; It shall not return to Me empty" (Isa. 55:11, NASB) led educators to believe that if people learned enough of the Bible, everything else would fall into line.

Christian Education

That was then...	This is now...
▲ Flannel graph	▲ Overhead projector
▲ Filmstrips	▲ Video
▲ Lecture	▲ Discussion
▲ Long-term commitments	▲ Short-term commitments
▲ One teacher	▲ Team teaching
▲ Evangelism-oriented	▲ Education-oriented
▲ Long attention spans	▲ Short attention spans
▲ Content-oriented	▲ Application-oriented
▲ Stress on form	▲ Stress on function
▲ Serve out of duty	▲ Serve out of need
▲ Public schooling	▲ Home or private schooling
▲ Functional families	▲ Dysfunctional families
▲ Rigid schedule	▲ Flexible schedule
▲ One education time	▲ Multiple education times
▲ Teach Bible knowledge	▲ Teach life skills
▲ Institutional-based	▲ Relational-based
▲ Facility-based	▲ Home-based
▲ Subject-centered	▲ Situation-centered
▲ Teacher-dominated	▲ Learner-dominated
▲ Didactic curriculum	▲ Relational curriculum

Unfortunately, this has not proven to be the case. Noting the research of Findley Edge, Edward Hammett wrote:

> But research has indicated even those of us who have been in church Bible studies all our lives are very poor students of the Scripture. If we know the cognitive material—that is the chronology of the narratives, or who the disciples were, or even to quote the books of the Bible or verses in those books—it impacts our daily lives very little.[3]

Today's Christian educators don't take for granted that Bible knowledge translates into Christian lives. They focus on applying biblical truth to individual lives.

2. Focus on the Learners

Where is the starting point in adult education? For years it has been the curriculum or the teacher. The student was expected to adapt to the subject, accepting or learning whatever the teacher or Christian education committee felt they needed to learn. Rarely did the teacher or the Christian education committee survey the adults to find out what they were facing during the week. Rarely were the needs of the student placed before the ideas of the institutional church.

Today this is reversed. Adults do not come to classes, services, or events that neglect their needs and interests. In past years adults came to church out of a sense of duty. Today if the class doesn't meet them where they are in real life, they stay home or go to another church that is meeting their needs. Out of necessity, then, the needs of learners are today's starting point for Christian education.

3. Growth of Christian Schools

Students who attend Christian schools receive an hour of Bible or other religious training every day. They are also highly motivated since they have to do the work to receive a passing grade. If a Christian school student must decide whether to spend time on a Sunday School lesson or a private school lesson for which they will receive a grade, guess where parents will encourage them to invest their time?

Christian school students who receive so much Christian education in their weekday curriculum find it boring to attend Sunday School just to hear another Bible lesson. The challenge of educating these highly knowledgeable students in Sunday School is great. But it is even more difficult where the Sunday School teacher has a mixture of public school students, who receive no Christian education at school, and Christian school students who receive so much. Sunday School teachers are finding that it takes more than reciting another Bible lesson to reach this group. These Christian school students do not need another lesson; they need to serve in some form of ministry.

4. Disintegration of the Family

The change of the family from an extended family to a nuclear family to a fractured family adds still another challenge to our times. Countering the breakdown of the home means more than providing a male role model for children without fathers. It means teaching children and youth the basic skills of life such as being polite, sharing, how to make decisions, etc. It means teaching parenting skills to those who never learned them from their own parents. It means teaching such skills to single parents. It means recognizing that families are couples with no children, single-parent families, blended families, divorced persons, and empty-nest couples.

5. Lack of Volunteers

Recruiting, developing, retaining, and training quality teachers who are committed and godly has never been easy. Just ask any person who has been a Sunday School superintendent; however, it is even more difficult in our changing times. Christian educators find that our fast-paced society immunizes people against a long-term commitment. People are suspicious of being trapped into a lifelong teaching assignment. Recruitment based on the needs of the institutional church lacks the inspiration it once did. Recruitment today takes on more of a relational style helping people find and use their spiritual gifts.

6. Broader Training Needs

With the breakdown of the family, many people have lost the place to learn the basic skills of life. Of course, Christian education will always focus on teaching the Scriptures, but in today's environment there is a growing need to train people in basic life skills. Christian education is focusing on integrating the Scripture with basic skills such as how to make decisions, communicate, negotiate, solve problems, think critically, be responsible, and maintain self-control.

7. Situation based Education

In years gone by, adult education classes focused primarily on the learning of content. This continues to be a need since many people are biblically illiterate. But some are attracted to Christian education more focused on the practical aspects of living rather than the pure acquiring of knowledge. For example, a person told us in one of our national seminars, "I'm more concerned about learning how to get through Monday than how the children of Israel got through the Red Sea."

8. Low-tech to High-tech

The days of teaching with a flannel graph, a slide show, or filmstrip are about gone. Children, youth, and adults are much more astute than these simple tools of a bygone era can provide. Even those who live in extreme rural areas have cable television or a satellite dish and a VCR. Video teaching is the wave of the future; and progressive churches already have invested in professional equipment to make their own videos.

9. Multiple Education Times

Along with the boom in multiple worship services has come the development of multiple educational times. In fact, one of the big challenges of adding an additional worship service is how to provide educational opportunities along with it. People in an exploding informational society like ours desire choices. They attend shopping centers with over 150 stores, eat at their choice of restaurants, and buy gas at a multitude of gas stations. They likewise prefer choices at church, and successful churches are offering more than one time for Christian education.

10. Off-campus Education

The growth in Christian education through the Sunday School in the 1950s was driven in part by the availability of cheap land and facility construction. Traditional Christian education was tied to facilities, and the growth of Christian education necessitated the construction of additional classrooms. This worked well until the 1980s when land and construction prices began to rise beyond the ability of many churches to handle. Along with this rise in cost was the growing adversarial relationship between Christianity and local governments. Today, growth in Christian education is moving away from a facilities orientation. Christian education takes place in small groups, two- and three-day retreats, and in short seminars held off campus in rented facilities.

Improving Christian Education in Changing Times

Often in Christian education ministries we think of teaching God's Word or providing fellowship for believers or to support Christians as they grow in their Christian lives. However, Christian education must begin to move outward by considering ways to reach today's seekers with the gospel of Jesus Christ.

1. Study the Trends in Society

Jim Williams, former vice president of the Baptist Sunday School Board (SBC) noted, "We need to take a fresh look at how people are behaving and acting, to provide a mirror for religious education to see what's good and what needs correcting." He further declared, "There has got to be an openness to change."[4] Take seriously the diversity and giftedness of your people and the uniqueness of your demographic location. Wyoming is not southern California; South Carolina is not New York; Texas is not Washington.

2. Evaluate Your Christian Education Ministry

The most difficult thing to change is what has worked well in the past such as Christian education. Our experience is that when something has worked so well, it receives little evaluation. So most churches' Christian education departments seem to drift along without much self-examination. The first step to improving your C. E. department begins with an evaluation. Think in terms of three areas: what was the past like; what is the present situation; and what should the future be?

3. Build Around Adult Needs

Research in the field of adult learning has found that adults learn best when they have a need to learn. Edward Lindeman observed, "In conventional education the student is required to adjust himself/herself to an established curriculum; in adult education the curriculum is built around the student's needs and interest."[5] What are the needs of adults? What are the needs of our people in their businesses, leisure times, families, communities, and clubs? Build your classes around the experiences, situations, and relationships adults are involved in. Adults learn best when they have to learn. Use the painful "teachable moments" of adult experience to teach them the Word of God. Help them cope with the hurts of life by holding the hand of God rather than running away.

The adults' experiences are perhaps the most important aspect of their learning. To understand and build Christian education of adults around their experiences in no way means to subordinate the Word of God to the experience of adults. On the contrary, it is to integrate the Scripture into the adult experience so that the experiences are understood and judged by the Scripture. All students of the Bible understand that the narratives of Scripture (particularly the Old Testament) are accounts of struggles and experiences of God's people. And they are written to us as an example: "Now these things happened to them as an example, and they were written for our instruction" (1 Cor. 10:11, NASB).

4. Communicate the Why of Education

Let your definition and philosophy of Christian education emerge or grow out of your people. Using a pre-written curriculum is fine, but adapt and customize it to your people and your philosophy. Individualize the learning experience for your own people. Remember that the best resources for adult education you will ever have are your own adults. Study, learn, and provide classes and learning experiences that fit the life situations and corresponding needs of your adults, and you will have a meaningful Christian education ministry. Adults learn best when:

▲ They want to learn;

▲ They understand why they need to learn something;

▲ They know the benefits of learning something; and

▲ They see how learning corresponds to what they are experiencing in their daily lives.

5. Structure Around Relationships

Walk into any adult Sunday School class and you can usually tell the age of the group which used the class by the seating arrangement of the chairs. Older classes will typically arrange the seats in straight rows which allow for a lecture style of teaching. Younger classes will typically arrange their seats in a circle or semi-circle to allow for more sharing. While it may not be completely true, many people perceive that small groups are relational and Sunday School classes are less relational.

The small-group movement has caused a fear among some adult Sunday School teachers. In some situations as small group attendance has risen, Sunday School attendance has declined. One reason for this trend is the desire of people for more relational settings and teaching. Christian education in our changing times needs to develop a relational style if it is to be effective in educating adults in the coming years. Today's younger generations are lonely and will be drawn to classes and groups which provide a sense of relationship.

6. Provide Ongoing Training

Equip Christian education workers by offering seminar-styled training. Be sure to include basic skills in teaching God's Word and leadership development. Make sure you provide training each year on practical ways to lead a child, young person, or adult to Christ.[6]

In designing your training process consider the following:

▲ Survey the church from the top down and bottom up. On a yearly time schedule ask the paid staff, leaders, teachers, and total congregation about their interests, needs, and concerns.

▲ Communicate the results of your survey to the key leaders.

▲ Tailor your training program to the needs discovered in your survey.

▲ Train people on the job so that they immediately apply what they learn.

▲ Recruit your best lay teachers and educators to train each other rather than having the paid educators training the unpaid.

▲ Continually redevelop your training program as the needs of people change.

7. Organize a Leadership Team

Carefully select a Christian education leadership team that will help you oversee the education ministry. Avoid the time-worn name of Christian Education Committee as it carries too much baggage from another era that was less relational in orientation.

Encourage the leadership team to inform your staff and church leaders of your workers' needs and concerns. Ask them to pray for all your Christian educators to be bold in their witness in the ministry God has given them. Cultivate the attitude of being alert to trends in Christian education. Study and interpret the trends affecting our society.

Make sure your leadership team focuses on developing excellent child care facilities and ministry. Keep a ratio of one adult to three children for proper care. Recruit couples and male nursery workers who can provide modeling for this vital ministry.

Use Dr. James Dobson's material called "Preparation for Adolescents" as a tool to reach pre-teens with important information as they change from child to young adult. In addition, provide training for parents to help them understand the changes that their adolescent children will be going through.

8. Begin New Classes

As classes grow, whether children, youth, or adult, give them inspiration to start new classes with the vision of reaching out to new people who need care and most of all the good news of Christ. As a rule of thumb, start another class for every fifteen pre-schoolers, twenty-five elementary students, ten teenagers, and thirty adults.

Remember that adult classes tend to reject the assimilation of newer people after about eighteen months of existence. If you hope to see newcomers joining your classes, you will need to start new classes at least every eighteen months.

9. Regroup Your Programs

The difficult economic times we live in have forced many businesses to consolidate in order to conserve resources and focus on what provides the most profit. Churches need to do the same. While we are not looking for financial profit, we do face a time when we have fewer resources of people's time and commitment. Therefore, we need to regroup our programs and focus on the ones that are honestly making disciples. Today's adults have less and less time which they are willing to devote to church activities. We can either be disgruntled about this change of events, or we can take a proactive stance and find ways to use them in the time they are willing to give us. Today's adults are not willing to attend even three events a week at the church, let alone the four or five events we often schedule. Of necessity, we must maximize the time we have them, even if it is only three hours a week. We must be intentional about those three hours so that they are the best three hours that we can give them.

10. Recruit Relationally

There are two styles of recruiting: institutional and relational. The institutional approach worked well when people served out of a sense of duty. It was based on the needs of the church and most often took the form of a "y'all come" announcement from the pulpit. People who responded were not given a ministry description and were likely to serve for many years in the same position.

Today people respond better to a relational approach which takes seriously their needs, interests, and gifts. Recruitment using this approach focuses on an individual interview to determine a person's gifts, talents, likes and dislikes of ministry, with the goal of placing the person into a ministry role which fits. Most often people are recruited for the short term, with ministry being renewed for the long term.

There's an old story about a woman who cut off the ends of her ham before she cooked it. After watching this ritual for years, her daughter asked, "Mom, why do you cut off the ends of your ham before you cook it?" After some thought, her mother replied, "I don't know. That's the way my mother did it, and I guess I've always followed her example." So they decided to call up Grandma and ask her why she cut off the ends of her ham. After asking Grandma, she told them, "Because I only had one pan, and I had to cut the ham to make it fit in the pan!"

The moral of the story, of course, is that sometimes we do things simply because we have always done them that way, not out of a sense of purpose.

The public education system is being forced to evaluate its organization and curriculum due to a changing environment which made the older forms of education obsolete. Change is the name of the game for Christian education also. While we certainly do not want to compromise the Scripture for the sake of relevance, we do need to understand the changes taking place and formulate a biblical response to Christian education in our changing times.

▼

NOTES

[1] Quoted by Dr. Haddon Robinson at the Tucson Perspectives on Ministry held in Tucson, Ariz., September 20, 1990.

[2] Letter quoted in *Illustration Digest* (Fayetteville, Ark.: Dr. Jon Allen, publisher, December-February 1992/3), 5.

[3] Hammett, citing Findley Edge's *Teaching for Results* (Nashville: Broadman Publishers, 1956), 13.

[4] Quoted by Edward H. Hammett in an article "Updating Adult Christian Education in Today's Southern Baptist Convention Church" published in *Christian Education Journal* (Glen Ellyn, Ill.: Scripture Press Ministries, Winter 1993), 11.

[5] Edward Lindeman, *The Meaning of Adult Education* (New York: New Republic, 1926), 8-9.

[6] Many of the major publishers such as Scripture Press, David C. Cook and Gospel Light will provide training for your workers. See the list of resources at the end of this chapter for addresses of several publishers. Also, most larger cities offer a Sunday School convention that will help train your workers.

RESOURCES

Seminars:

Fellowship of Christian Educators, ON-345 Willow Rd., Wheaton, IL 60187; (708) 665-4667.

Journals:

Christian Education Journal. Available from Scripture Press Ministries, P.O. Box 650, Glen Ellyn, IL 60138.

For Further Reading:

Aleshire, Daniel. *Faithcare: Ministering to All God's People Through the Ages of Life.* Philadelphia: Westminster Press, 1988.

Anthony, Michael J., ed. *Foundations of Ministry: An Introduction to Christian Education for a New Generation.* Wheaton: Victor Books, 1992.

Clark, Robert E., et. al. *Christian Education: Foundations for the Future.* Chicago: Moody Press, 1991.

Davis, Ron. *Mentoring: The Strategy of the Master.* Nashville: Thomas Nelson, 1991.

George, Carl F. *Prepare Your Church for the Future.* Tarytown, New York: Fleming H. Revell Co., 1991.

Schaller, Lyle E. *Create Your Own Future.* Nashville: Abingdon Press, 1991.

Resources for Training:

Accent Publications, 12100 W. Sixth Ave., Box 15337, Denver, CO 80215; (800) 525-5550 or (303) 988-5300 (in Colorado).

David C. Cook Publishing, 850 N. Grove Ave., Elgin, IL 60120; (800) 323-7543.

Gospel Light Publications, Box 6309, Oxnard, CA 93031; (800) 446-7735.

Group, Box 481, Loveland, CO 80539.

Scripture Press Publications, 1825 College Ave., Wheaton, IL 60187; (800) 323-9409.

Standard Publishing, 8121 Hamilton Ave., Cincinnati, OH 45231; (800) 543-1301.

13

*The Christian church is not exactly known
for setting trends or embracing change.*
     —George Barna

*The only thing we know about the future
is that it will be different.*
     —Unknown

GOOD NEWS–BAD NEWS

During World War II, the *Lady-Be-Good* was a bomber whose crew was a well-seasoned team, a group of intelligent and combat-ready airmen. After a successful bombing mission, they were returning to home base late one night. In front of the pilot and copilot was a panel of instruments and radar equipment they had to rely on to reach their final destination. They had made the flight many times before, so they knew about how long it took to return.

But this flight was different. Unaware of a strong tail wind that pushed the bomber much more rapidly through the night air than usual, the men in the cockpit looked in amazement at their instruments which correctly signaled it was time to land.

The crew, however, refused to believe those accurate instruments. Confident they were still miles from home, they kept flying and hoping, looking intently for familiar lights below. The fuel supply was finally depleted. The olive drab bomber never made it back. It was found deep in the desert many miles away. The crew perished, having overshot the field by a great distance because they followed their feelings which "seemed right" but proved wrong.[1]

What happened in the air back in the early 1940s is happening in many churches today. Good, sincere, well-meaning, intelligent people continue to pursue ministry with methodologies and programs which once worked well, but today are not as effective.

It's a good news–bad news type of situation. The good news is it is the mid-1990s and there is great opportunity for ministry. The bad news is many of our church people still think it is the mid-1950s and are not taking advantage of the opportunities facing them.

Five Ideas That Didn't Come True

"Everything that can be invented has been invented."
—Charles H. Duell, 1899, Director of the U.S. Patent Office

"Sensible and responsible women do not want to vote."
—Grover Cleveland, 1905, President

"There is no likelihood man can ever tap the power of the atom."
—Robert Millikan, 1923, Nobel Prize Winner in Physics

"Heavier than air flying machines are impossible."
—Lord Kelvin, c. 1895, President, Royal Society

"Babe Ruth made a big mistake when he gave up pitching."
—Tris Speaker, 1921, Baseball Player

New Models of Ministry

Any approach for communicating the changeless Word of God involves three elements: the *truth* to be shared, a *technique* for delivering the truth, and a *target* audience to receive the truth.

As an example of this, think back to the early 1950s when the Youth for Christ rally was an effective technique for reaching youth with the gospel. The truth was the gospel, the technique was the rally, and the target audience was youth.

This approach to winning youth to our Lord was very effective. Unfortunately, over the years, teenagers began to change; competition from television and other recreational activities emerged; and the YFC Rally lost its effectiveness. The gospel hadn't changed; the YFC Rally hadn't changed; but teenagers had changed.

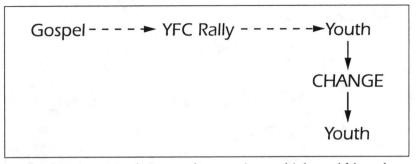

In this situation there are three options which could be taken. The first is to keep doing what has always been done and miss the target audience completely.

Option #1: Ineffective

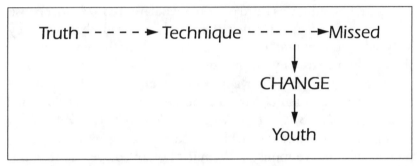

The second option is to change the truth, which is obviously unacceptable.

Option #2: Unacceptable

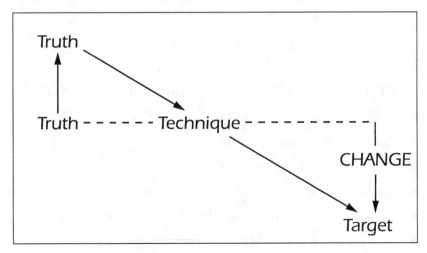

The third and best option is to change the technique.

Option #3: Effective and Acceptable

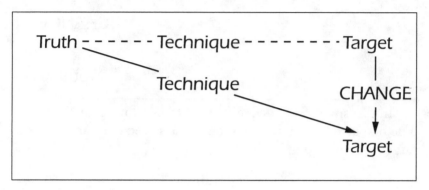

To their credit, this third option is what Youth for Christ chose to do. After recognizing that their audience had changed, they adapted their program to meet the new needs of the new teenagers they wanted to reach with the gospel.

The only aspect of our approach which is unchanging is the truth. The Bible points out that the Lord Jesus Christ does not change (Heb. 13:8) and His Word does not change (1 Pet. 1:25).

Pastors and church leaders are under pressure to develop new models of effective ministry. We must not, of course, sacrifice the gospel on the altar of trends; but we must creatively adapt, integrate, and communicate the Word of God to a changing audience.

New models must be developed that fit the new values of people in our society. Some values we must keep in mind as we plan for the future are these:

▲ Time is more important than money.

▲ Quality is more important than quantity.

▲ Effectiveness is more important than tradition.

▲ Variety is more important than limited selection.

▲ Application is more important than facts.

▲ Flexibility is more important than ritual.

▲ Casualness is more important than formality.

▲ Choices are more important than single options.

▲ Acceptance is more important than separation.

Making Changes

With these changing values in mind, here are some insights for designing change in your church.

Insight #1: Develop High-Touch Ministries

"High Tech–High Touch" is the buzz word of the information age. A university study found that students were able to retain information longer in a library when librarians lightly touched the students' arms while answering questions. Churches should:

▲ Place an emphasis on relationships.

▲ Expand small groups.

▲ Use counseling centers.

▲ Train members in the Stephen Ministry.[2]

Insight #2: Offer a Variety of Ministries

M.O.P.S. (Mothers of Preschoolers), Divorce Recovery, and Never Married Singles groups are a few of the new ministries being developed in many churches. New ones are continually needed. Churches should:

▲ Employ workers who are specialists in their fields.

▲ Manage specialized workers the way a conductor leads an orchestra.

▲ Target new ministries to new groups.

▲ Deploy ministries away from the church facilities.

Insight #3: Remain Flexible

People are busy. Yesterday a husband would come home from work to a prepared meal. Today he finds a note on the kitchen counter that reads, "Honey, if you get home before I do, please start dinner." Churches should:

▲ Conduct alternate services.

▲ Expand opportunities throughout the week.

▲ Hold a Friday or Saturday evening service.

▲ Shorten services.

Insight #4: Establish a Clear Purpose

The demands of keeping a church going often take precedence over its basic purpose. However, ideas do not come from information but from conviction of purpose that burns in the heart and spreads to others. Churches should:

▲ Clarify their purpose.

▲ Present things in concrete terms rather than philosophical ones.

▲ Increase ownership through regular communication.

▲ Explain their purpose in real-life stories.

Insight #5: Keep It Simple

Pastors labor under the misconception that it is better to have too much information than too little. Psychologist George Miller found almost twenty-five years ago that only seven pieces of information, such as digits of a telephone number, can be held easily in a person's mind for short-term memory. Churches should:

▲ Simplify everything.

▲ Make sermons clearer and shorter.

▲ Make traffic patterns, instructions, and signs obvious.

▲ Announce only what is of interest to everyone.

Insight #6: Practice Good Communication

A survey done by the Opinion Research Corporation found that fewer than half of employees rated their companies with favor when it came to letting them know what was going on in the company. Executives rate communication problems as the chief difficulty. Churches should:

▲ Tie communication to images.

▲ Use stories. Half of our learning is fact; the other side is stories and ideas.

▲ Use humor. Research suggests that putting people in a good mood by telling them jokes helps them think through their problems with creativity.

▲ Communicate everything five different ways.

Insight #7: Be Patient

Churches are taking more time to make decisions. They are being more careful and taking the time to search for additional information. Pastoral search used to take three to six months; today it takes nine to twelve months. Churches should:

▲ Ask good questions.

▲ Set criteria for decision making before beginning research.

▲ Use decision-making grids.

▲ Look for consensus rather than unanimous decisions.

Insight #8: Trust Others for Advice

There is an inability to keep up with produced information. Leaders must accept the fact that they can't know it all. Broadman & Holman Publishers releases around sixty-five books each year but receive around fifteen hundred manuscripts annually! Churches should:

▲ Use consultants. They have a broader base of experience and understanding to interpret information.

▲ Ask questions.

▲ Don't wait forever to make a decision. You will never have all the information you would like.

Insight #9: Focus on Application

People only remember 15 percent of what they hear. George Simmel, a sociologist, was the first to recognize that in urban life people protect themselves from information overload "which results in an incapacity . . . to react to new situations with the appropriate energy." Churches should:

▲ Focus on known information rather than dumping more information.

▲ Tell people how.

▲ Concentrate on the basics.

▲ Preach and teach topically.

Insight #10: Emphasize Long-term Growth

People are being forced to adapt to a new life pace. They must confront novel situations and master new ways of doing things in ever shorter intervals. Churches should:

▲ Develop home Bible studies which teach people to find information for themselves.

▲ Limit information to what people really need to know. "Everything I Really Need to Know I Learned in Kindergarten" is true.

▲ Use a variety of teaching techniques. Not everyone learns the same way.

A few summers ago, we had the opportunity of visiting the United States Olympic Training Center (OTC) in Colorado Springs, Colorado. The OTC is home to many of our Olympic offices as well as the site of one of the most up-to-date training centers available.

One of the interesting training areas was the one used for rifle target practice. A large room allows for shooting at targets from as close as fifteen meters to as far away as fifty meters. The fifty-meter target can be used for both stationary and moving targets.

The moving target is a picture of a boar, which moves steadily across the end of the room as competitors try to hit a target on its side. How does a person hit such a moving target?

One can aim behind the boar and, of course, miss it altogether. One can aim directly at it and, due to its movement, may only hit the back end of the boar. Or one can aim just in front so that the boar moves into the line of sight at the right moment to be struck by the bullet.

How do you hit a moving target? By aiming in front of the target!

How are we to hit the moving target of effective ministry in our changing times? By keeping alert to the movements in our culture and aiming our ministries just slightly ahead of them so we touch the lives and hearts of people.

Are we effectively seeking and saving the lost? Are our ministries changing lives? Are people becoming obedient to the faith through our churches? If so, we are hitting the target. If not, perhaps we need to shoot a little more out front.

▼

NOTES

[1] Charles R. Swindoll, *Stress Fractures* (Portland, Oreg.: Multnomah Press, 1990), 176-177.

[2] For information contact Stephen Ministries, 8016 Dale, St. Louis, MO 63117-1449; (314) 645-5511.

RESOURCES

Anderson, Leith. *A Church for the 21st Century.* Minneapolis: Bethany House Publishers, 1992.

Barna, George. *What Americans Believe,* 1991; *The Frog in the Kettle,* 1990; *User Friendly Churches,* 1991. Ventura, Calif.: Regal Books.

George, Carl F. *Prepare Your Church for the Future.* Old Tappan, N. J.: Fleming H. Revell Co., 1991.

Hunt, Josh. *Let It Grow! Changing to Multi-Congregational Churches.* Grand Rapids, Mich.: Baker Book House, 1993.

Schaller, Lyle E. *It's a Different World: The Challenges for Today's Pastor.* Nashville: Abingdon, 1987.

Walrath, Douglas. *Leading Churches Through Change.* Nashville: Abingdon, 1989.

Other Able Assistants
for Your Ministry. . .

Power House:
A Step-by-Step Guide to Building a Church that Prays

The 12 Essential Skills for Great Preaching

Eating the Elephant:
Bite-sized Steps to Achieve Long-term Growth
in Your Church

The Issachar Factor
Understanding Trends that Confront Your Church and
Designing a Strategy for Success

This bonus section offers help from several specially chosen assistants in the Broadman & Holman group of professional books. The excerpts that follow have been chosen from our other Professional Development Books to give you helpful insights on additional subjects of particular interest to ministers.

Power House:

A Step-by-Step Guide to Building a Church that Prays
by Glen Martin & Dian Ginter

In *Power House*, you'll learn how to unleash the power of prayer—the single most effective force for energizing a church. You'll discover how to assess your congregation's prayer skills and develop a step-by-step strategy for renewal and outreach based on prayer. *Power House* also includes inspiring examples of churches transformed by prayer.

A well-oiled machine is a joy to behold—intricate parts of all sizes and shapes, close together and yet working smoothly as one. However, the very parts that were designed to work together in perfect, close harmony will tear each other up without proper lubrication. So it is in the church.

Prayer—God's Oil for Relationships

God has provided the wonderful "oil" of prayer, which if properly applied, can help all members work together in spite of the differences. Prayer provides the lubrication so that as a church, made up of different parts, all members can fit together perfectly, working together without friction to perform a job which they could never accomplish on their own.

The same principle is true of the component parts of the church. When heavy-duty prayer is applied, the various leadership elements—deacons, trustees, councils, laity, mission groups, etc.—can work in harmony. This means prayer that is enough to saturate the decision-making process, not just a "drop" of prayer at the beginning of a meeting, not just token praying for relationships that do not reach the need, but in-depth praying that not only reaches the needs, but also applies God's oil to the problems, to the points of friction that would otherwise damage or destroy things of value. This really means the whole machine needs oil on an ongoing basis.

Looking further at this illustration, in the world of machinery different kinds of oils—various grades and different weights—are used for a specific need. To apply too light an oil when a heavy-duty one is needed can lead to trouble. Too heavy an oil where a light one is called for may gum up the works or be overkill.

The same concept applies to prayer. There are different kinds of prayer for different kinds of situations. God has shown us how to pray for certain results, confess when appropriate, intercede for others, and do spiritual warfare in specific situations. Each fills a need and, when used appropriately, can be the very oil to make our lives and our churches run their best.

A powerful house of prayer is a church that knows the value of the oil of prayer. It is using prayer to maximize all of its ministries and to maintain a smooth running operation. Prayer is acting as a shield against any of the enemy's attacks on all ministries and relationships.

Prayer Ministry vs. House of Prayer

At this point a distinction should be drawn between having a prayer ministry and desiring to be a house of prayer. A prayer ministry involves a portion of the congregation in ministry, as with a youth ministry. A limited number will be involved—usually, those with a greater burden for prayer. Such a ministry may take the form of missionary prayer circles; times of prayer open to the whole church such as a Wednesday night prayer meeting; or men's/women's/youth's prayer meeting; a prayer room; an intercessory team; prayer ministry before/during/after the church service; or a prayer chain. In such cases, prayer will be seen as something done by some but not all of the membership. It will be just another, although important, ministry, as is evangelism or choir.

Some churches have tried to solve this problem by creating a prayer room in their facility, thinking this is the equivalent of becoming a house of prayer. The prayer room can be a very helpful component of the prayer life of a church but should not be the main focus. It is only a part of the overall prayer picture.

All prayer ministries are important for they lay the foundation for becoming a house of prayer since there is already an acknowledgment of the strategic importance of prayer in the church. God will help you build on your current ministry and help you go to the next level of prayer, until you truly become a powerful house of prayer.

The 12 Essential Skills for Great Preaching

by Wayne McDill

Wayne McDill's book teaches specific preaching skills like painting word pictures, bridging from text to sermon, exploring, exploring natural analogies and much more. He offers you the opportunity to privately critique yourself and improve your skills in a way that is most comfortable for you.

Strengthening Preparation Skills

He made it look so easy. Michael Jordan could run headlong down the court, bouncing the ball on the floor while several other men tried to get in his way, then leap into the air with others clamoring about him and cause a pumpkin-sized ball to slip through a steel hoop as easily as dropping a lump of sugar into your coffee. We celebrated his skill by cheering, and through him we felt some fleeting sense of personal accomplishment. I wish I could do that.

I listened to Itzhak Perlman play a Mozart violin concerto and marveled. He closed his eyes and, in his characteristic way, seemed to delight in every note, his facial expressions animated as though he were singing through the violin. I was caught up in his performance and found myself moving with the flow of the music. I wish I could do that.

But I cannot play basketball like Michael Jordan or the violin like Itzhak Perlman. Neither can you. What do they have that you and I do not? Why can they perform their crafts the way they do while we are only skilled enough to watch? In the first place, they have the gifts for it. Built into the genetic formula for these two very different men is the treasure of a giftedness few people have.

Another difference between these two men and the rest of us is the time and effort they have put into developing those gifts. While you and I were watching television as children, Michael Jordan at the same age was dribbling and shooting baskets. Itzhak Perlman was practicing his scales and double stops. They invested their freedom in disciplined practice of their skills while most of us were using up our freedom with something else. Now they have the freedom to perform as one in a million can, while the rest of us are not free to do that.

Factors in Skills Development

No matter what our gifts, everyone needs help. My guess is that somebody, somewhere along the way, helped these two stars with their training. Jordan and Perlman were taught the basic dynamic principles of their crafts, the technique for every skill they would need. Then they practiced. They practiced hours. They practiced devotedly. They were probably driven to practice insatiably while other young people were making softer decisions about their time.

Not only am I not good at basketball or the violin, neither am I good at a host of other activities. Why? It takes time. I heard Robert Schuller say in a pastors' conference, "I determined early in my ministry that I could not afford to be good at golf. You have to choose what you will be good at, because you can be good at only a very few things." What have you decided to be good at? If you have the gifts for performing well at it, then you must develop the skills associated with those gifts.

The premise of *12 Essential Skills* is simple: Preachers can significantly improve their preaching by strengthening twelve specific skills used in the preparation of sermons. Skills development means the gradual growth in your skills in a particular craft, in this case preaching. Here we concentrate on twelve tasks which are necessary to the most effective sermon preparation.

It is important to understand the basic concepts behind the skills you are learning. If you understand why something is done, you are more likely to remember how it is done. The skills necessary for effective preaching are based on the principles of biblical interpretation, sermon structure and development, language use, and communication. The better a preacher understands those principles, the more sense the particular skills he needs will make and the more likely he will be to understand the role particular skills play in the work of sermon preparation.

Skills development training requires hands-on experience working with the material of a given craft. You will never develop skills in a particular work just by hearing about it. You have to be a doer and not a hearer only. This will involve an understanding of the properties of the raw material with which you work. If it is basketball, you have to get a feel for the ball and the basket. In the case of sermon preparation, the raw materials are ideas and language, particularly in the words of the text and of your sermon. You are a wordcrafter, handling the words of Scripture and the words of communication. So you have to get the feel of words—judging what they can do and cannot do, exchanging them, matching, and assembling them for the best results.

Skills are learned best when they are first explained in practical, step-by-step terms. The skills for any performance involve concrete actions that must be accomplished in a certain order. This requires clear instructions. Learning how to do anything is much easier if the task is broken down into achievable steps which can be taken one at a time. If you don't have a personal coach, written instructions should be clear enough for reference and reinforcement as you continue to practice.

Skills development must take into account that each person comes to the task with different experience, background, and expertise in the particular skill. So it is with the development of preaching skills. It is important that you work at your own pace and level. If you are already skilled in a particular task, you will want to move on to other skills you need to strengthen. Different preachers also have different levels of giftedness, creativity, and potential. It is best to deal with the basics while allowing plenty of room for creative freedom as you go along.

Skills development calls for modeling of the particular tasks so the student can see how it is done by an experienced craftsman. No matter how clear instructions may be, a few good examples are necessary. It is best to have a coach present to demonstrate the particular task you are learning. Less effective is a written example. As you work at strengthening sermon preparation skills, you will need not only instructions, but examples showing what the task looks like on paper.

In skills development there is no substitute for practice. Just because you think you understand something doesn't mean you can do it. Practice is the only way to master a skill, even in sermon preparation. This means writing, writing, writing. Completing a task one time is not practice. At first the work may seem tedious, and you are uncertain. But as you keep working with different texts, you will find yourself more and more at home with each task. Do not work at one preparation task for more than three or four hours at a time. After that you may become mentally fatigued and perhaps frustrated with the task. Regular and consistent practice over the weeks is better than too much at once.

Eating the Elephant

**Bite-sized Steps
to Achieve Long-term Growth in Your Church
by Thom S. Rainer**

Eating the Elephant shows why, in many cases, "contemporary" church growth plans can do more harm than good. It also explains how the long road to lasting growth is best traveled in tiny steps—through creating sensitive change at a comfortable pace.

Most pastors realize that some type of change must take place in their churches in order to reach effectively a growing unchurched population. Many pastors face two major obstacles: lack of know-how and the inability to apply known principles of change.

Generally, innovations can be implemented with relative ease in three cases: (1) a newly-planted church; (2) a church that has experienced rapid growth due to relocation; or (3) a church that still has its founding pastor. Churches in these three categories account for less than 10 percent of all Christian churches in America. What do the remaining 90-percent-plus churches do? Can they be effective? Can they make a difference in their communities? Can they reach the unchurched? Can they implement change without destroying their fellowship?

Such is the tension that exists in many of the so-called traditional churches. How can the church be relevant to both the growing unchurched population *and* to the members for whom church relevance is grounded in old hymns and long-standing methodologies? The good news is that the traditional church *can* grow. Through my contact with hundreds of such churches in America, I have discovered that many pastors *are* leading traditional churches to growth. I will share with you their principles and struggles. And I will share with you my own successes and failures of leading traditional churches to growth.

Many of my church members know that I love a good, clean joke. One of them shared with me a series of elephant jokes. One of the jokes asked the question: "How do you eat an elephant?" The answer: "One bite at a time." Later I would realize that the joke describes well the task before any leader in a traditional church. The process of leading a traditional church to growth is analogous to "eating an elephant." It is a long-term deliberate process that must be implemented "one bite at a time."

If the task before us is eating an elephant, then we must avoid two extremes. The first extreme is to ignore the task at hand. I remember when my son Sam had a monumental science project to complete. He was overwhelmed by the enormity of the task. Working together, we established a list of items to be completed and the date by which each item had to be finished. Instead of being a burden, the project became a joy because he could see his daily progress. Much to his amazement and delight, Sam finished the assignment several days before the deadline.

If we acknowledge that our churches are far from effective, the challenge to change may seem overwhelming. You are in the same situation as most pastors in America. But with God's anointing, you can lead toward change and growth one step at a time.

On the other hand, we must avoid the other extreme of eating the elephant in just a few bites. Massive and sudden change (I realize "massive" is a relative term but, for many church members, their "massive" is the pastor's "slight.") can divide and demoralize a traditional church. Remember, church members who hold tenaciously to the old paradigms are not "wrong" while you are "right." They are children of God loved no less by the Father than those who prefer a different style.